WHAT I MEANT WAS

NEW PLAYS AND SELECTED ONE-ACTS

WHAT I MEANT WAS

NEW PLAYS AND
SELECTED ONE-ACTS

CRAIG LUCAS

THEATRE COMMUNICATIONS GROUP

This publication is made possible in part with public funds from
the New York State Council on the Arts, a State Agency.

TCG books are exclusively distributed to the book trade by Consortium
Book Sales and Distribution, 1045 Westgate Dr., St. Paul, MN 55114.

Due to space constraints, the copyright page and
credits for cited material continue on page 309.

LIBRARY OF CONGRESS CATALOGING-IN-PUBLICATION DATA

Lucas, Craig.
What I meant was : new plays and selected one-acts /
by Craig Lucas. —1st ed.
p. cm.
ISBN 1-55936-159-X (alk. paper)
I. Title.
PS2562.U233 W48   1998
812'.54—dc21   98-49478
CIP

Book design and typography by Lisa Govan
Cover design by Chip Kidd
Cover painting is *The Expulsion from Paradise* by Masaccio (1401–1428),
and was provided courtesy of Scala/Art Resource, NY

First edition, June 1999

ETERNAL THANKS TO MY AGENT,

PETER FRANKLIN—A GENTLEMAN

AND A SHARK

CONTENTS

CONTENTS

I'M TRYING TO MAKE A BABY with a friend. We're not inti-
mate partners. How will we work out all the details? Eighteen
years—such a long commitment. What if we are not up to the
task? What if the child grows to hate us for making such an
unconventional home—a straight, deaf, single mom and a
gay, hearing, single dad who do not share a domicile?

Putting out this edition of plays from the last several
years seems allied to the risk entailed in making this baby. It
is, after all, a terrible world in which very large beasts run
rampant. The ignorance and provincialism of the culture of
theatre, particularly in New York, seem a mild analogy to
what this child will encounter past the walls of that unconventional and sprawling home we're attempting to build.

The forces of reaction would have us believe that my
friend and I are attacking the sanctity of families, and the
cultural critics would have me believe that I have failed in
the writing of these plays, because they did not garner the
commercial success of one earlier play.

Both of these ideas come to me bereft of hope. To my
unborn, unconceived child, and to the readers of these plays
I say:

We are ever more than they want us to be, fully alive here in our disheveled moment.

But agency is ours. Who said it had to be their way?

These plays were written to be performed, not merchandised. And children are born to make their own world, not populate a replica of a nonexistent past.

To the future—theirs and ours.

—CRAIG LUCAS
April 1999

THE DYING GAUL

For Tony Kushner

An earlier version of *The Dying Gaul* was produced at the Citizens Theatre in Glasgow, Scotland, on March 19, 1998. It was directed and designed by Jon Pope. Lighting design was by Michael Lancaster and music was by Adrian Johnston. The cast was as follows:

ROBERT	Stephen Scott
JEFFREY	Henry Ian Cusick
ELAINE	Lorna McDevitt
FOSS	Stephen MacDonald
MALCOLM	Jay Manley

The Dying Gaul opened on May 31, 1998 at New York City's Vineyard Theatre, Douglas Aibel, Artistic Director, Jon Nakagawa, Managing Director. Scenic design was by Allen Moyer, costume design by Jess Goldstein, lighting design by Christopher Akerlind and original music and sound design by David Van Tieghem. It was directed by Mark Brokaw. The cast was as follows:

ROBERT	Tim Hopper
JEFFREY	Tony Goldwyn
	(replacing the injured Cotter Smith)
ELAINE	Linda Emond
FOSS	Robert Emmet Lunney

Woe to him who seeks to please
rather than to appal.

—HERMAN MELVILLE
Moby-Dick

■ ONE ■

Robert alone.

ROBERT: "Self-salvation is for any man the immediate task. If a man lay wounded by a poisoned arrow he would not delay extraction by demanding details of the man who shot it, or the length and make of the arrow. Begin now by facing life as it is, learning always by direct and personal experience."

———

Jeffrey's office. Jeffrey and Robert.

JEFFREY: So, Robert . . . do people call you Robert or Bob?
ROBERT: Both.
JEFFREY: Which do you prefer?
ROBERT: I don't . . . I sort of like to see which they prefer and then that tells them something, tells me something about them.
JEFFREY: I gotcha. Interesting. You're a very good writer.
ROBERT: Thank you.

(Pause.)

JEFFREY: What kind of movies do you like? You like movies?
ROBERT: Oh yeah.
JEFFREY: You do. What are some of your favorite movies?
ROBERT: Oh, you know, I like all kinds of movies.
JEFFREY: You do.
ROBERT: Oh yeah, I like, you know, movie movies, and I like old movies and foreign movies.

(Pause.)

JEFFREY: What was your favorite movie last year?
ROBERT: Last year? I don't really go in for favorites, you know, I sort of think each movie, like each painting or book or . . . national park . . . is actually unique and to be appreciated as such, god I sound like an English professor, I like . . . I liked very much . . . um . . . I thought that, uh . . .
JEFFREY: That's okay.
ROBERT: No, I liked that English—*Remains of the Day*, and I loved the dinosaur movie. I mean I like all uh . . . every thing along the continuum.

(Short pause.)

JEFFREY: Well, we're interested in your script.
ROBERT: What?
JEFFREY: We're interested in *The Dying Gaul*.

(Short pause.)

ROBERT: Okay.
JEFFREY: So. That's that . . . *(Short pause)* Your agent is . . . ?
ROBERT: Dead.
JEFFREY: Oh.
ROBERT: Yeah. Malcolm Cartonis.
JEFFREY: I'm sorry.

(Pause.)

ROBERT: Yeah.

JEFFREY: Who's . . . ? . . . taken over for him?

ROBERT: Well, nobody, unfortunately, he was kind of a one-man band . . .

JEFFREY: Well, a good one, obviously, because he got us the script and I read it and Kohlberg's read it.

ROBERT: He has?

JEFFREY: Yes. We don't greenlight anything without his approval.

ROBERT: Greenlight?

JEFFREY: No, I'm not saying we're making your script, I'm saying we've all read it and we all think it's good . . . and that's why I'm talking to you.

(Intercom buzzes.)

Yes?

WOMAN'S VOICE: Your wife.

JEFFREY: All right. *(To Robert)* Excuse me. *(Into receiver)* Hi . . . Sure . . . Sure . . . Sure . . . Sure . . . Okay. Love you too. *(He hangs up)* Where do you think you want to go with the script?

ROBERT: I'm sorry?

JEFFREY: Where else do you want to go with the script?

ROBERT: Well, I . . . I guess I could take it to some of the independents.

JEFFREY: No, no, no . . . what a doll you are. What kind of work do you want to do on it?

ROBERT: Oh. Oh, sorry . . .

JEFFREY: That's okay. That was just so sweet. From acceptance to total rejection, you took it all in stride. What kinds of things have you thought about, or do you think it's finished as it is?

ROBERT: Well, it's as far as I could take it without some sort of input from a director.

JEFFREY: Uh-huh. And who's your dream director?

ROBERT: Oh, Gus Van Sant, I guess. Since Truffaut's dead.

JEFFREY: Good. He's very good. Would you like me to show him the script?

ROBERT: Yeah, sure, why not?

JEFFREY: Good. 'Cause I already have. And he likes it.

ROBERT: Do you have any smelling salts?

JEFFREY: You're really very charming. He likes it very much, and he has some questions as we all do, and . . . who knows if he's the right person or not, but I wanted to talk to you first before we set up a meeting. What's the title, explain the title to me.

ROBERT: Well, you know, they go to that museum in Rome . . .

JEFFREY: Ken and Maurice.

ROBERT: . . . and they see the sculpture . . .

JEFFREY: Yeah, yeah, yeah, but why is that the name of the movie?

ROBERT: Because. Oh, I see, because they feel that the statue is depicting the, like, the defeated, the vanquished:—

JEFFREY: Uh-huh.

ROBERT: . . . and dying soldier, and the Gauls fought naked and without armor—

JEFFREY: Right.

ROBERT: —so he's so young and defenseless . . .

JEFFREY: Beautiful.

ROBERT: With just this little hole in his side . . . otherwise . . . and being that the statue is *by* a Roman, by one of those whose side was responsible for all the slaughter, it would be like an American making a statue honoring the suffering of . . . one of the countries we've fought, a person from . . .

JEFFREY: From where?

ROBERT: One of, whatever countries we've invaded, not invaded. You know what I'm saying. Like . . .

JEFFREY: Okay, so, Ken and Maurice see this sculpture of this . . . Gaul. Who is dying . . . And?

ROBERT: And they identify with the Gaul in a way because they're gay and so many of their friends are dying and they keep looking for some kind of response from the enemy . . .

JEFFREY: Right?

ROBERT: And then remember where they talk about the sculpture and say . . . "Well, what good did it do the poor guy who bled to death, the guy in the—?"

JEFFREY: Right. Right.

ROBERT: "But at least . . . maybe . . . some kind of compassion was awakened in the Romans, and maybe at some time in the future as a result of someone *seeing* the sculpture, maybe some other . . ."

JEFFREY: Gaul.

ROBERT: ". . . was, somebody took pity or spared some other French peasant from . . ."

JEFFREY: Yeah, I get it. That's very . . .

ROBERT: It's kind of oblique.

JEFFREY: No, I understand, and it has a political overtone.

ROBERT: That's right. Which I imagine . . .

JEFFREY: No, no, we're not afraid of that, we're not afraid of anything, the idea, obviously, is to reach as many people as possible and to have the broadest appeal, so that we can make money, but also so that . . . to whatever degree the movie effects people, it can also serve as a kind of Dying Gaul for the viewers. I mean, if you even look at a movie like . . . well, say, just to pick something, *Tootsie*, which we didn't make but which is a very good movie—

ROBERT: It's a great comedy.

JEFFREY: It says something . . . in a small, but totally amusing way . . . and you don't see it coming: about men and women. The guy is an arrogant . . . you know, chauvinist, and he, for his own reasons, dresses up, feels he has to dress up as a woman, and as a result, he learns something about what it means to be a man. He finds, it's so obvious, if you know it's there, but he finds a feminine side to himself and vows: you don't actually see it happen, but you know he does it—

ROBERT: Uh-huh.

JEFFREY: —he vows not to be such an asshole, and you feel good for him.

ROBERT: Yeah.

JEFFREY: So that's the kind of political statement you can slip an audience without their feeling they've been had or they're being lectured.

ROBERT: Right.

JEFFREY: And . . . Well, *The Dying Gaul* isn't a comedy, it's a weepie, what I call—Like *Terms of Endearment*. And these movies are *Very. Hard. To sell.*

(Pause.)

ROBERT: Uh-huh.

JEFFREY: They're *Very. Hard. (Pause)* And they're my favorite kind of movie. They just have to be made with care. And . . . *The Silence of the Lambs* is another one which touches on feminist ideology without . . . Did you like that movie?

ROBERT: Yes and no.

(Short pause.)

JEFFREY: Okay.

ROBERT: Did you make it?

JEFFREY: No, no. No, no . . . Why didn't you like it?

ROBERT: The, uh, faggy portrayal of the killer.

JEFFREY: He's not gay. Jamie Gumb is not gay.

ROBERT: Yeah, that's what I heard, but I think that's a bunch of bullshit. Because he has the poodle—

JEFFREY: I had a poodle. My wife and I had a poodle.

ROBERT: Yeah, but I bet you don't wear nipple rings and put on eyeliner and, you probably don't cut up women because you want to be one.

(Pause.)

JEFFREY: You never know.

ROBERT: True.

(Short pause.)

JEFFREY: So what are we gonna do? Do you want to sell this
   script?
ROBERT: Sure.
JEFFREY: And . . . do you want to do the rewrites?
ROBERT: Well . . . what do you mean?
JEFFREY: I mean . . . are you interested in doing the rewrites
   or do you want to sell the script outright?
ROBERT: I don't . . . *Of course.* I don't want somebody else . . .
JEFFREY: Okay.
ROBERT: . . . mucking around with this—
JEFFREY: Good. Great. I'm glad you're . . . I'm sorry you
   don't have an agent, though. Are you going to sign
   with somebody else?
ROBERT: Oh, I don't know, Malcolm was a really close friend
   and . . . *(Short pause)* I haven't been able to find another
   agent.

(Pause.)

JEFFREY: We can deal directly with you. Or recommend a
   lawyer. Oh, I should let Business Affairs call you, we
   should stick to the artistic discussion. They'll offer you
   more than minimum, so, with the rewrites, you know,
   this could be a couple hundred thousand, but . . . don't
   let that sway you. What? . . . Okay, so . . . I understand
   your reasons for wanting the men to be men, because
   of the political dimension, but . . . Ken and Maurice.
ROBERT: I'm not making them heterosexual.
JEFFREY: No, no. *Please.*
ROBERT: I'm sorry.
JEFFREY: No, I mean, I understand . . . I read your script,
   Robert, I know what kind of person you are.
ROBERT: I'm sorry.
JEFFREY: I'm not asking you to jettison any of your principles.

(Pause.)

ROBERT: Sorry.

JEFFREY: We like. Your script.

(Intercom buzzes.)

Hold all my calls.

(Silence.)

What . . . Presumably you are looking for something universal . . . in the experience of two gay men . . . which a wider audience can identify with.

ROBERT: You could say that.

JEFFREY: Would that be a true statement? . . . Okay. You want to reach as many people as possible with the universal human . . . *truth* about these two characters. One of whom is a Person With AIDS. Now. Don't. Say. Anything . . . until . . . Okay. Most Americans. Hate. Gay people. They hear it's about gay people, they won't go.

ROBERT: What about *Philadelphia*?

JEFFREY: *Philadelphia* is about a man who hates gay people. Period. And it's been done. To get people into the theater, the movie theater, they have to think it's going to be fun. Or sensational. Or . . . some kind of—make them feel fantastic about themselves. No one. Goes to the movies. To have a bad time. Or to learn anything. To be improved. Do we agree with this?

(Pause.)

ROBERT: Yes.

JEFFREY: What is important is what they leave the theater with. Yes? . . . And if they don't . . . *enterrrrrr* . . . the theater, they don't get a chance to leave it. Is this all acceptable to you . . . as a thesis? *(Pause)* No one is going to see *The Dying Gaul*. If you make it with Tom

Cruise—who wouldn't go near it for a hundred million dollars, oh fuck, he'd blow me and you for a hundred million dollars, but you know what I'm saying, and with . . . Clint Eastwood . . . and got Steven Spielberg to direct it and released it in two hundred million screens . . . No one. Is going. To see. *The Dying. Gaul. (Pause)* I am sorry. Now. If we make Maurice a woman dying of AIDS, and let's face it, heterosexuals are also getting AIDS, in disastrous numbers—

ROBERT: I want nothing to do with this.

JEFFREY: We'll write our own script based loosely on *The Dying Gaul*—

ROBERT: Fine.

JEFFREY: Or we'll give you one million dollars for your script.

(Pause.)

ROBERT: A million dollars?

JEFFREY: With which you can go out and write four hundred new screenplays about men with, gay men with AIDS, without AIDS, a gay love story, whatever is the most important to you.

ROBERT: If you want the script so much—

JEFFREY: We think it is good. Robert. We want to make your script, and we will pay you for it. We will not make *The Dying Gaul* with two men in bed, falling in love, surviving pain and all the blah blah blah, it's not going to happen. Ever. Ever. Ever. I will guarantee you the first rewrite, *twice* scale, because you are a wonderful writer, with a beautiful visual sense, and a realistic understanding of forward action, which is not nothing, and an appreciation of the innate laws of storytelling as it directly relates to movie-making, and there are about mmmmmaybe twenty of you. In the world. We want your script. We want you to rewrite it.

ROBERT: This is so . . .

JEFFREY: I know. Sit down. *(Pause)* Please? You don't have to stay, or agree, you just, you could listen.

ROBERT: Ohhh . . .

(Pause.)

JEFFREY: There can be minor characters who are gay. They
don't have to be gags.

ROBERT: Oh, they can be noble, right?

JEFFREY: They don't have to be noble. They can be whatever
you want. They cannot be the center of the story,
because the center of the country is not gay and the
center of the country is what pays for the movies to be
made.

ROBERT: The center of the country isn't black, either, but
they made *Malcolm X.*

JEFFREY: Yes. In fifty or twenty-five or maybe even who knows
how many years we can make the gay version of *Malcolm
X,* and people will go, but they will not go now in 1995,
and how we know this is empirical observation.

(Pause.)

ROBERT: Were you serious about the million dollars?

JEFFREY: Are we having a conversation, Robert—

ROBERT: I'm going to take the script to Paramount—

JEFFREY: Yes, we are serious about the million dollars.

ROBERT: Somebody wants to be in my movie. Who wants to
be in my movie?

JEFFREY: I told you that Gus Van Sant is interested, he has
not committed—

ROBERT: Oh come on, you're not gonna let Gus Van Sant
direct this movie until he makes a giant blockbuster
which he will never do—

JEFFREY: He might.

ROBERT: —and you'll fire him before we ever go into production and bring in Joel Fucking Schumacher.

JEFFREY: It's not a bad idea, you know, and he's gay!

ROBERT: *Who wants to be in the movie?* Tell me now or it's a
million and a half.

JEFFREY: Tom Cruise and Michelle Pfeiffer. And Denzel Washington, Martin Sheen, Jim Carrey and Winona Ryder, Meg Ryan, Daniel Day Lewis, Debra Winger and Johnny Depp . . . among others. I wish you would sit.

ROBERT: Word travels fast. Who wants to play Maurice?

JEFFREY: They all want to play Maurice, but we can work that out.

(Pause.)

ROBERT: You have virtually no idea how much one million dollars would mean in my life. I live in a basement apartment which floods when it rains, because I am still paying off my college loan. I have a son for whom I pay child support, and Malcolm who just died, my agent, was also my lover.

(Pause.)

JEFFREY: I'm sorry.

ROBERT: I can't in good conscience . . . take this money from you.

JEFFREY: You are an amazing and lovely person, Robert, and you have succeeded in making me feel like a total scumbag.

ROBERT: Good. I'm glad.

(Pause.)

JEFFREY: How's your health?

ROBERT: It's okay. I'm negative.

JEFFREY: Good.

ROBERT: Yeah, I check it every two seconds, Maurice and—I mean Malcolm, god oh god, Malcolm and I always had safe sex. Can't I write you a new script, something altogether—

JEFFREY: We want *The Dying Gaul*, and we want you to write it. Take the million and write something else.

(Pause.)

ROBERT: Oh Jesus . . .
JEFFREY: Yes?

(Pause. Robert nods.)

(Into the intercom) Liz, would you call Albert in Business Affairs and ask him to come on down here, please, give me two minutes. *(Pause)* Congratulations. You are a millionaire. *(Pause)* Do you want to see the brand-new Mike Leigh? Have you seen it?
ROBERT: No.
JEFFREY: Are you interested?
ROBERT: Sure.
JEFFREY *(Into the intercom)*: Liz, would you arrange a private screening for this evening with Robert Isaacson and me for the Mike Leigh, then book a table at Spago for ten-thirty— *(To Robert)* You have plans?
ROBERT: No. No.
JEFFREY *(Into intercom)*: And call my wife and tell her I have to work late, please, tell her I'll call her from the restaurant. *(Pause)* You're very talented, and very lucky, and so are we. I feel good about this, Robert . . . I want you to feel good. *(Short pause)* Yes? *(Pause)* What's wrong?
ROBERT: I can't really . . . I can't say.
JEFFREY: What? Tell me? *(Short pause)* Hey. Hey. Hey. Hey. It's going to be a beautiful movie, and you are going to write more movies, and some day . . . you are going to be able to write your own. Ticket. Do you . . . Look at me. I mean that . . . I mean that, Robert. Look at Spike Lee. He makes movies he cares about . . . About his own people. And they make money. And that will happen. For you. I want that for you. Come here . . . Give me a hug.

(They hug.)

Okay?

(Robert nods.)

You are very very handsome . . . And I'm getting . . . a little . . . turned on . . . Are you? *(Short pause)* You can do anything you want. As long as you don't call it what it is. You understand?

———

Robert alone.

ROBERT: "The first fact of existence is the law of change or impermanence. Life is a bridge, therefore build no house on it. Whosoever clings to any form, however splendid, will suffer by resisting the flow."

———

Jeffrey's home. Robert, Elaine and Jeffrey.

ROBERT: So beautiful.
ELAINE: Well, spend a few hours driving around up here in the canyon and nearby, you'll sneer at us.

(Short pause.)

ROBERT: But your garden.
JEFFREY: Two seconds, sorry!
ROBERT: These incredible bromeliads.
ELAINE: You know plants?
ROBERT: Some. Malcolm, my lover who . . .
ELAINE: Yes.
ROBERT: Was obsessed with herbs and all flowers, he knew everything.
ELAINE: You have a garden?
ROBERT: Well, I have the remnants of what he left in a, oh, it's a little fenced-in plot behind my apartment; when he was really sick, I, he would tell me what to pull up, when to water . . . Now it's . . .

ELAINE: I don't have a single idea what all this is, the gardener put everything in, I planted these couple of lettuces and mâche or these edible flowers—

ROBERT: Nasturtium.

ELAINE: —in between, so I could make fresh salads, which I hardly ever do.

ROBERT: You should, I think you should be careful about—

JEFFREY *(Overlapping to Elaine)*: Offer him something to drink.

ROBERT: I think this here might be monkshood—

JEFFREY: Baby?

ELAINE: What can I get you to drink?

ROBERT: Oh, gosh, I feel I should say spring water, but I'd really like a vodka.

ELAINE: Peppered? Lemon? Ketel One?

ROBERT: Oh, I'll drink 'em all and we'll stay all night. Just a plain . . . But you know—

ELAINE *(Overlapping)*: Up?

ROBERT: Sure. But . . . you should . . .

(Elaine exits.)

Some of these . . .

(Jeffrey is on hold.)

JEFFREY: Some view, huh?

ROBERT: Oh god.

JEFFREY: There are days I can't believe, I wake up early or come home especially late— *(Into the phone)* Uh-huh? Okay. *(He hangs up)* I'll look out and think: I live here. This is actually my home. When is someone going to march in and demand the keys back . . .

(He kisses Robert, gropes him.)

ROBERT: Should . . . ?

JEFFREY: It's okay. I want to suck you until there isn't a drop of juice left and then lick you from head to toe . . . and . . . and have you inside—

(Elaine returns.)

—the foreign markets and video, you'll be able to have a second house looking down on *us* . . .

ELAINE: Oh, everyone looks down on us, that's nothing. What part of town do you live in, Robert?

ROBERT: Oh god. I live in West Hollywood in a rental.

JEFFREY: Not for long.

ROBERT: Oh, I don't want to change anything, not for now. I don't want to get used to . . .

ELAINE: Oh, you will. Elevator going up! Up and up; the context shifts, things you thought were luxuries become essential . . .

ROBERT: Uh-huh.

ELAINE: Suddenly your decisions are . . . *informed* by your desire to own *another* Balthus.

JEFFREY: Darling. He's just made the first money he's ever seen in his life, he's paying child support and alimony, he's not thinking about . . .

ELAINE: No? Take a look at *Faust*, that's all I'm saying. Decide for yourself.

JEFFREY: They told me not to marry Cassandra, but I don't know, she seemed so . . . prescient.

(Pause.)

ELAINE: How many kids do you have?

ROBERT: One. We had him the second it was clear to both of us that our love was probably not gonna make me straight, and I think we thought in that . . . idiotic way of our . . . fear and twenty-four-ishness . . . that . . .

ELAINE: Oh, but you must love him.

ROBERT: Oh yeah, but . . . Yeah, of course. He's . . . he's my life now. He and his mom live in New York.

(Pause.)

ELAINE: I'm sorry about your friend. *(Short pause)* When did he die?

ROBERT: January.

ELAINE: Of this year?

ROBERT: Uh-huh.

ELAINE: So you're still . . .

ROBERT: Uh-huh.

ELAINE: Oh god.

JEFFREY: . . . Rough.

(Pause.)

ROBERT: Sides of me . . . things I didn't know were there have sprung up . . . taken over.

ELAINE: Such as?

ROBERT: Oh, I'm like famished, you know, for distraction.

ELAINE:	JEFFREY:
Such—	Well, I mean, that—it stands to reason.

ROBERT: Oh . . . the computer.

ELAINE: I just got my first.

ROBERT: Oh really?

JEFFREY: As we limp into modernity . . . the last on the block to have e-mail at home.

ELAINE: I hear it's already passé, I'm so . . .

ROBERT: Oh, not to me. Send me e-mail, I'll answer, I sit all day, days in a row—surfing the Internet?

ELAINE: Do you do those chat rooms? *(To Jeffrey)* What?, he doesn't have to answer.

ROBERT: No, I don't mind. I love them. Actually. They're like life after death, I think . . .

ELAINE: How so?

ROBERT: There's all these voices, you know?

(Jeffrey's cell phone rings.)

. . . these disembodied . . . souls . . .

JEFFREY *(Into phone)*: Yeah . . . Oh, fuck him . . . *Fuck* him . . . No, tell him I said it . . . I'm perfectly—This is, okay—

ELAINE: Go on. Please.

ROBERT *(Simultaneously)*: No faces, no cor—

JEFFREY *(Simultaneously)*: This is my message: Fuck you, Scott. Fuck—If he asks—

ELAINE: Jeff!

JEFFREY: —why I'm angry, tell him I said "Fuck. You."

(Jeffrey's conversation continues, unheard.)

ROBERT: Sorry. No corporeal being at all—

ELAINE: Uh-huh.

ROBERT: . . . floating in this . . . *place* where, that doesn't even exist, really . . . You . . . only touch in the sense that you see a reflection of them and they see some sort of reflection of you, but only what you want them to see: it can be the most essential part of you, but that's your choice, you know?

ELAINE: Well . . . not really; I haven't seen them, I've only heard.

ROBERT: I mean, well, the Buddhists—You know anything about Buddhism?—Buddhists believe that the only thing after life is the cumulative effect of our actions: karma, and that's what it's like, all this karma just colliding in the middle of *nowhere*—

(Jeffrey hangs up and reemerges.)

ELAINE: Uh-huh. But I'm interested in hearing about the sex part.

JEFFREY: Of course you are, and that's why we love you, more vodka, Robert?

ROBERT: No. Yes, please.

ELAINE: You want to, hey, you want to see my . . . *lllllaptop?*

ROBERT: Sssssssure.

JEFFREY *(Overlapping)*: Oh, great.

(Jeffrey exits; Elaine gets her laptop.)

ELAINE: I can't figure out a fucking thing about this thing . . .
Jeffrey's busy making his . . . twelve figures and my kids
are too young . . . The guy—

ROBERT: Oh, wow, look at this.

ELAINE: Is it good?

ROBERT: Well, it's kind of a Silver Cloud compared to my
used bicycle.

(Jeffrey returns with bottle of vodka.)

JEFFREY: Let me just say that we have to be relatively sober,
or I do, by the time the scores come in after the screening . . .

ELAINE: I hate hate hate hate these screenings.

JEFFREY: You don't have to go.

ELAINE: I hear about a project for years sometimes and never
meet the writers until we go to the mall. I think they
should spell it M-A-U-L. So I insisted on meeting you
before I had to see you completely crestfallen—whenever your movie does get made—shaken, trembling,
cast aside. And Jeffrey made you sound like there was
a glint of a human being in there, so I had to see for
myself. Watch everyone's faces when the scores come
in. Just *watch*.

JEFFREY: It isn't—

ELAINE: The harder the writers have struggled to keep some
sort of sense or artistry or meaning in their story—

JEFFREY: It—

ELAINE: —the worse the picture does, always, because Jeffrey
is always right . . . *(To Jeffrey)* Hm?

JEFFREY: Nothing.

ELAINE: Maybe as a Buddhist you won't be so susceptible to
all that.

JEFFREY: You're a Buddhist?

ROBERT: Well . . .

ELAINE: So show me how to get on-line. Oh, I'm already on.
Rob131?

ROBERT: I signed on as your guest.

ELAINE: So this is the name you use . . . ?

ROBERT: Sometimes. You can have as many names as you want.

ELAINE: You can?

ROBERT: Make up a completely different profile.

ELAINE: So for every facet of your personality . . . ?

ROBERT: Exactly.

ELAINE: Mmmm. So how do we get to the really filthy rooms?

JEFFREY: Yeah, I want to see, too.

ELAINE: I can sign on, and that's about it.

ROBERT: Okay, let's see, click on MEMBER rooms—

ELAINE: And then you see peoples' members?

ROBERT: Well, you can, actually, I mean, you know, people send naked photos . . . Here, I like this room, *Men4MenParkBench.*

ELAINE: Park bench?

ROBERT: Yeah, you know, you pretend you're sitting on or sometimes under or maybe, you know, walking by a park bench and then . . . stuff happens . . .

ELAINE: How?

ROBERT: What do you mean?

ELAINE: What happens?

JEFFREY: Nothing, that's the point: safe sex.

ELAINE: But, okay, can I just ask how you type and do that at the same time?

ROBERT: Well, you alternate.

JEFFREY: Isn't this nice we're all getting to know one another so fast?

ROBERT: So you can click on someone's name—

ELAINE: *ILove2Lick!?*

ROBERT: —and check their profile.

JEFFREY: We gotta go, kids.

ELAINE: "Investment banker. Affectionate, tactile, roMANtic"—

JEFFREY: Gotta go.

ELAINE: "Discreet, no guy can be too hairy" . . .

JEFFREY: I agree, but we can just make it in time if we—

ELAINE *(Overlapping)*: "My idea of a quickie is the entire weekend"—

JEFFREY *(Continuous)*: —leave now—

ELAINE: "Let me teach you the Vulcan Lip Lock!" No wonder you—

JEFFREY: All aboard that's going ashore!

ELAINE *(Continuous)*: —want to do this all the time—

JEFFREY: Elaine—!

ELAINE *(Overlapping, exiting)*: I gotta pee, you're the boss, Jeff, Jesus, you've kept me waiting often enough! *(She is gone)*

JEFFREY: She insisted. She had to meet you. Least this way she won't suspect.

ROBERT *(Mouthed)*: SH!

JEFFREY: No, we had cork put in every room so we could be loud as we liked, Max and Debbon couldn't hear us when we came. FUCK ME, ROBERT, COME ON! INSIDE ME! *(His voice low again)* She likes you. She really does. She's just playful and . . .

ROBERT: I like her.

JEFFREY: She's incredibly smart and frustrated and . . . unfulfilled and . . . working on herself and I really couldn't live without her and I really can't wait till the movie starts so I can feel your dick in my hand . . .

(Elaine returns.)

ELAINE: Were you calling me?

JEFFREY: Nope, let's go.

ELAINE: Thank you for showing me your secret world, Robert, I appreciate it.

ROBERT: It was nothing.

JEFFREY: Come!

———

Jeffrey's home. Elaine alone.

ELAINE: The screening turns out to be surprisingly interesting, a project Jeffrey fought for under the old head of production—and the scores are good, and we all ride back together and laugh and celebrate our new friendship and their joint project, and after we drop Robert off, after we get back and put the children to bed and Jeffrey and I have made love, he was unbelievably *excited*, Jesus, it's . . . it's a little . . . well, it's new having him enthusiastic about . . . another human being . . . not just sex, I mean, but . . . and it's another, possibly one more part of his life I won't get to share in. Oh, I know Jeff likes men. And I've never minded what doesn't threaten . . . us. But . . . the way he kissed me . . . just now . . . I have to find some way in, a means to join in whatever it is they . . . have or don't have . . . A way— *(Pause)* Well, I don't have to decide what it is I'm going to do exactly, do I? I find my little on-line manual . . . with the house dark and all of the valley stretched out and flickering like phosphorescent fish, the tiny lights on the sound system and the fax machine, the security system, the pool, the walkways, all the faint glowing electric underpinnings of our lives which hint at the excitement I feel as I figure out how to make up a new screen name . . . and sign on now as: *(Types into her laptop)* Skinflute7. Profile: "33. Venice Beach. Landscape architect." Find my way to *Men4MenParkBench*. I know he has to have a more salacious moniker than *Rob131*, but is it one of these? *MrThick*: "Medical professional." *HornyZack*: Favorite quote: "If I blow your mind, you have to promise not to think in my mouth." I don't think so.

JEFFREY *(From off)*: Come to bed!

ELAINE: I'm checking my e-mail, I'll be in! *(Pause)* HotHand-Sm: "If you're not happy with what you have now, how can you be happy with more?" *He* certainly doesn't work in Hollywood. *DGBottom*. Dig—? DogBottom? Quote: "The purpose of life is the attainment of Enlightenment . . ." Blah, blah, "the process consists in

becoming what you are, look within, thou art Buddha."
Thank you. *(She types)* You are in *Men4MenParkBench*.

(We hear overlapping voices murmured in the darkness:)

FOSS:	ROBERT:
I haven't tasted a cock in three and a half years.	Big juicy uncut dick ready to be serviced.
JEFFREY	FOSS:
What's up?	Like UR handle.

ROBERT: Me, frankly.
JEFFREY: Me too. Wanna call me?
FOSS *(Overlapping)*: Real cannon when it goes off, huh?
ROBERT *(Overlapping)*: Can't give out my number.
FOSS: Wanna call me?
JEFFREY: Can't give out my number.
FOSS *(Overlapping)*: Can't give out my number.

(The voices drop in volume, whispers under:)

ELAINE: Like entering a warm bath. And he's right: it is like
life after death . . . a din of restless souls searching for
the impossible, contact where there is no flesh. *(She
types and enters an Instant Message)* "Hi Guys!"
FOSS: —two fingers, you're moaning, acting like you're just
checking out the scenery—
JEFFREY: Hi, Skin.
ELAINE: Hi there, *Bubba*.

(A little ping sound.)

ELAINE: Oh, I got an Instant Message:
FOSS: Can I play your flute?
ELAINE: Oh, go away. *(She types)* Anyone here ever lost a
friend or a lover?
JEFFREY: —plowing your hole—

FOSS: You're in the wrong room, Skin, go to keyword "Grief," you'll find all sorts of bulletin boards and support groups.

JEFFREY: Good luck!

FOSS: You'll get through it.

(Another ping. Robert and Elaine begin exchanging Instant Messages:)

ROBERT: I have.

ELAINE: Dogbottom! Yes. I can barely type, my fingers are shaking so badly. *(Her IM)* It's only been a feq—a *few* weeks.

ROBERT: It gets worse.

ELAINE: I can't believe he said that, what if I'm suicidal? *(An IM to Robert)* I think I may be suicidal.

ROBERT: I was, too. It's good you're telling someone.

ELAINE: I think about it all the time.

ROBERT: I do, too. But you need to see a professional, it's imperative.

ELAINE: Imperative, he's assuming I'm smart. *(To Robert)* Do you still think about killing yourself?

ROBERT: Yes.

ELAINE: Do you picture how you'll do it?

ROBERT: I know how I'll do it.

ELAINE: How?

ROBERT: It's painful, and I don't want to give you any ideas. See a shrink!

ELAINE: Where do I find someone? *(Aside)* Saying anything to keep him on the hook . . .

ROBERT: Call the lesbian and gay hotline.

ELAINE: I don't just want anybody.

(Short pause.)

ROBERT: They'll refer you to several people.

ELAINE: He loves to help, doesn't he? *(Her IM)* Did you go to a shrink?

ROBERT: Yes, I still do.

ELAINE: Where did you find them?

ROBERT: Oh, my boyfriend and I saw him together for couples counseling when he first got sick. He'd already been seeing him for years. Tell me about your lover.

ELAINE: He's beautiful, very muscular, *before*. I still talk about him in the present tense.

ROBERT: Of course.

ELAINE: Do you do that?

ROBERT: Sometimes. How did he die?

ELAINE: God. *(To Robert)* TB.

ROBERT: Mine too.

ELAINE: Really?

ROBERT: Was he on the protease inhibitors?

ELAINE *(Aside)*: Jesus— *(To Robert)* . . . Yes, but it was too late. Yours?

ROBERT: No.

ELAINE: Why not?

ROBERT: His doctor said he didn't qualify for any of the trials.

ELAINE: I C.

ROBERT: But I should have tried harder—gone to the underground, bribed somebody or broken into a lab—anything . . .

ELAINE: You did everything you could, I'm sure.

ROBERT: You don't know that.

ELAINE: You sound like a very loving guy, I'm sure you did. *(Pause. Aside)* I don't know where I'm getting half of this, but— *(To Robert)* Did you help him die? *(Silence. Aside)* Shit, wrong. *(To Robert)* Hello?

ROBERT: Did you help yours?

ELAINE: Yes. *(Aside)* Sure, why not?

ROBERT: You did?

ELAINE: He asked me to. You?

ROBERT: Can't say.

ELAINE: Why?

ROBERT: Don't really want to.

ELAINE: Okay. *(Aside)* I'm blowing it.

ROBERT: Yes. I did. *(Short pause)* You're the first person I've told. My shrink doesn't even know. No one.

ELAINE: Wow . . . My grief has me thinking I'm losing my mind. Is that natural?

ROBERT: Yes.

ELAINE: What can I expect?

ROBERT: The worst.

ELAINE: I've been like . . . crazy for sex.

ROBERT: That sounds about right.

ELAINE: What does one do?

ROBERT: Well, if you're me, you trawl these rooms half the night and sleep with all the wrong people.

ELAINE: Like?

ROBERT: Like people you have no business fucking.

ELAINE: Like me?

ROBERT: That's right, it's too soon.

ELAINE: You don't want to fuck me?

ROBERT: See a shrink!

ELAINE: I will, please don't go.

ROBERT: Okay.

ELAINE: It would feel so good to have someone here . . . Have you started dating again?

ROBERT: Not really.

ELAINE: Just sex.

ROBERT: Right.

ELAINE: Who's the last person you slept with? *(Pause)* It turns me on to hear people tell their experiences.

ROBERT: Oh . . . I met this guy through work?

ELAINE: What kind of work do you do?

ROBERT: I'm a writer.

ELAINE: Go on.

ROBERT: And he's straight or says he is, and he's got kids.

ELAINE: Wow. That's hot.

ROBERT: And he likes me to fuck him.

ELAINE: So what's wrong with that?

ROBERT: He's my boss on a project.

ELAINE: I C.

ROBERT: Yeah, so . . . see a shrink.

ELAINE *(Aside)*: He rode with me in my car and laughed at my fucking jokes . . . an hour ago.

ROBERT: Hello?

ELAINE: Did you find yours through the hotline? *(Aside)* Where am I going with this?

ROBERT: No, he was recommended by a friend.

ELAINE: And he's really good?

ROBERT: Yes. But lots of people are good, you'll find the right one.

ELAINE: I'm afraid I'll get someone who just happens to have a lot of free time, I'm desperate. *(Aside)* Nothing comes back, he's debating whether it's ethical to give me his shrink's phone number.

ROBERT: I'm sure my shrink can recommend someone really good, I'm seeing him tomorrow; can I e-mail you?

ELAINE: Can't I call him direct? *(Pause)* Again, he's thinking, and in that instant it all comes clear: what I *could* do if I wanted to know more about him—this man my husband— *(Pause)* If I wanted to know everything about him . . .

ROBERT: Dr. Michael Foss, he's in Beverly Hills, in the book, say I said to call for a reference.

ELAINE: Thank you! My name's Sean, by the way.

ROBERT: Robert. *(Short pause)* And you're welcome! *(Short pause)* 'Night.

ELAINE: Night. Thanks again. X—X—X.

(Elaine alone.)

Perfect and complete, like an egg, it falls at my feet . . . all I have to do is pick it up. Jeffrey says it's simply a matter of what you give yourself permission to do: and there are no limits to what you can accomplish . . . Assuming you can pay, he leaves that part out . . . That's all it ever comes down to, isn't it?

———

Foss's office. Robert and Foss. Foss takes notes.

FOSS: Who do you want to kill? *(Pause)* This is a dream of annihilation.

ROBERT: Me.

(Pause.)

FOSS: Jeffrey?

ROBERT: No, he's the guard. He's the Nazi.

FOSS: You're the prisoner. *(Short pause)* What is Jeffrey to you?

ROBERT: He's . . . oh . . . *money.* Success. I guess I don't deserve those. Why? I beat you to it. Because Malcolm is dead. And Jeffrey is—Oh, he's fine, he's actually very hot, you know? I like to get him off. It's touching, you know, his clothes, the expense of just about every inch of him, the . . . wanting to be degraded.

(Short pause.)

FOSS: When were you a Nazi? *(Silence)* When did you have to bark orders at an emaciated, dying . . . ?

ROBERT: Oh. Yes. I did . . . sometimes. Of course, he wouldn't want to eat, and he had to, he wouldn't want to take his pills. Even if he would throw them up—"Then take them again, I don't care if it feels good, I don't care if you want to, I'm telling you, I'm not asking you." . . . He'd . . . Once . . . he said something like, "Okay, I'll take them, I'll eat, but promise me . . ." God . . . He said: "Just . . . you have to *use* this, make it count for something. All this—a script or a novel."

(Jeffrey enters.)

JEFFREY: Congratulations. You are a millionaire.

(Jeffrey exits.)

ROBERT: I broke my promise.

FOSS: Oh. So you should die. No one else: you. You should pay more. You haven't suffered enough, you should keep—

ROBERT *(Simultaneously)*: Okay, okay.

FOSS *(Simultaneously)*: —paying more. *(Pause)* What is attractive about Jeffrey? What excites you?

ROBERT: . . . He has no scruples. He does what he wants, whatever he wants, he goes after it. No fear. He loves his wife, but that isn't all he wants, he wants kids and a family, but he also wants adventure, and he loves to get fucked.

(Jeffrey enters.)

JEFFREY: She doesn't have a cock, that's all, it isn't her fault. Now can we not—?

ROBERT: Well, but couldn't, I mean, she could . . . stick something in there, you don't need me.

JEFFREY: I like men, I like women, I like you and I want you to fuck me. Please?

FOSS: Why is that attractive? . . . Tell me if I'm wrong, but I think there is something else.

(Pause. Cellular phone rings, and Jeffrey moves to answer it as before.)

JEFFREY: Yeah . . . Fuck him.

ROBERT: Oh.

JEFFREY: *Fuck* him.

ROBERT *(Simultaneously)*: His anger.

JEFFREY *(Simultaneously)*: No, tell him I said it—I'm perfectly—This is, okay, this is my message: Fuck you, Scott.

ROBERT: He doesn't hold it in at all. He's incredibly—

JEFFREY: If he asks why I'm angry—

ROBERT: It's impressive.

JEFFREY: —tell him I said, "Fuck. You."

(Jeffrey exits.)

FOSS: Who do you want to see thrown in the gas chamber?

ROBERT: No one. *(Pause)* I don't *feel* it, I'm sorry.

FOSS: You dream of a Nazi concentration camp . . . Who do you know who's Jewish?

ROBERT: I'm not mad at you.

FOSS: Malcolm? . . . Who's responsible for his death? . . . Whose job was it to save him?

ROBERT: Mine. If I could have gotten him on the protease inhibitors?

FOSS: Why was it your job? What about his doctor?

ROBERT: Oh, what a lost cause, he's a total burnout, he can't remember which patient is which.

FOSS: Why wasn't it my job?

ROBERT: . . . You were away.

FOSS: And where's your anger about that?

ROBERT: You left me the morphine, I could have used it.

FOSS: But you threw it away, after I explicitly asked you to return it. You weren't angry. *(Short pause)* Why didn't you call me when I was in Fiji?

ROBERT: Oh, yeah, you were going to fly back . . . "Hi, how's the beach, sorry to interrupt your mai tai, but Malcolm's dying, bye."

FOSS: Who did you want to throw in the dumpster along with the morphine? . . . Who were you *killing*—? Who did you want to kill? Who *did* you k—

ROBERT: All right, all right! . . . It didn't work. The morphine didn't work, it didn't stop his heart . . . Jeeze. *(Short pause)* His heart went right on beating, bam bam bam bam!

(Short pause.)

FOSS: You used it.

ROBERT: Directly into his port. Yes. It didn't work.

FOSS: Five months after the fact you're just now getting around to telling me this—?

ROBERT: It's my loss, not yours. Mine. *(Short pause)* Malcolm was mine.

FOSS: So you've kept him to yourself all this time.

ROBERT: His heart was really strong, he'd grown used to the morphine, that's all, it wasn't your fault. I know you loved him.

FOSS: This isn't about my feelings.

(Silence.)

ROBERT: I have to let him go.

FOSS: Not without rage. It don't work that way. Sorry. *(Short pause)* What would you say to him? If he were here. Look at him, he's right here, tell him:

(Jeffrey enters.)

JEFFREY: Fuck me.

ROBERT: I'd—

JEFFREY: Fuck—

ROBERT: I'd sa—

JEFFREY: You.

(Short pause. Robert checks his watch.)

ROBERT: I guess we're—

FOSS: That's all right. Think about what you would say to him, if you could. Talk to him. *(Short pause)* It's important that you be careful. *(Short pause)* If you think you need to be punished . . .

JEFFREY: Fuck me.

FOSS: . . . people walk in front of traffic . . .

ROBERT: I see.

FOSS: They have unsafe sex. *(Pause)* No one needs to be punished.

(Short pause.)

JEFFREY: Fuck.

FOSS: Especially—

JEFFREY AND FOSS: You.

ROBERT: Uh-huh.

FOSS: God . . . God needs to be punished . . . Kill god. Or me. In your mind's eye . . . Kill . . . *Malcolm*.

JEFFREY: Congratulations.

ROBERT: Yes.

Foss alone.

FOSS: Robert should see someone else, I'm too close to it. I want to refer him to someone, and the only reason I'm waiting, I want to make sure I'm doing it for the right reason. Yesterday when I came in, I noticed several objects on my desk were out of place; and files were out of order, Robert's files. Had I put them in the wrong place? Was I trying to get rid of him, lose him? Or had someone been here? Nothing is missing: artwork, valuable laptop, easily carried out. The fact that I'm even thinking someone could have gone through files, photocopied—it's an indication, to me at least, of how deeply ambivalent I am about being seen: exposed for what is in that very file . . . The mere *suspicion* of a break-in here and the possible breach of a patient's confidentiality should be enough for me to have gone to the police. But again: the possibility, however remote, someone would find a reference to my having helped Robert and Malcolm in that selfsame file which I had, yes, myself uncharacteristically misfiled. Was that my wish? To be found out, to be punished for daring to toy with a life? I could lose my license. So this is my fear; that I'm wanting to get rid of Robert, fob him off on someone else, refer him, wipe him away, so I don't have to face him: this weekly, painful reminder of my own . . . inefficacy? And if you think sitting with that kind of grief is a picnic . . . *(Short*

pause) "Learn to do good, cleanse your own heart."
This is the teaching of the Buddhas. *(Pause)* We'll see.

––––––

Jeffrey's home; Robert's apartment. Elaine and Robert are onstage in their respective homes. They are both at their computers. We hear the men's voices as voice-overs—murmured, indistinct, overlapping one another, a wash of words:

JEFFREY: That's it, babe, talk to me . . .

ROBERT: Shoot.

FOSS: Tell me 'bout that BIG STRONG COCK fucking your hand . . .

JEFFREY: Now that's a "loaded" question.

ROBERT: Give me your load.

FOSS: Salty. You taste salty.

JEFFREY: What is that gorgeous eight-inch dick doing right now?

ROBERT: Warm, wet pussy hole . . .

FOSS: Come on . . . I want to make you come.

(Suddenly, an Instant Message:)

ELAINE: Hi, DG!

ROBERT: Hi.

ELAINE: Can I sit beside you?

ROBERT: Sure.

ELAINE: Do you mind if we just talk?

ROBERT: No.

ELAINE: Sometimes, having sex without getting to know someone is a little weird.

ROBERT: I agree.

ELAINE: Not weird, but unsatisfying.

ROBERT: Yes.

ELAINE: How are you feeling?

ROBERT: Okay.

ELAINE: Are you sure?

ROBERT: Well . . . more or less.

ELAINE: You seem sad.

ROBERT: Do I know you?

ELAINE: Yes.

ROBERT: I'm sorry, I don't remember our chatting.

ELAINE: Look at my name.

ROBERT: Arckangell?

ELAINE: That's me.

ROBERT: You're an angel?

ELAINE: Yes, I am.

ROBERT: Does that mean you do nice things, that what makes you an angel?

ELAINE: That's part of it.

ROBERT: And we've talked before?

ELAINE: Yes.

ROBERT: Did you have a different name?

ELAINE: Yes.

ROBERT: What was it?

ELAINE: If I tell you, you'll go away.

ROBERT: No I won't.

ELAINE: Yes, trust me, you will.

ROBERT: Okay. So . . . did we have sex?

ELAINE: Yes.

ROBERT: More than once?

ELAINE: Yes.

ROBERT: Really?

ELAINE: Yes.

ROBERT: Okay. Tell me what I like.

ELAINE: You are extremely versatile. You like kissing most of all. Am I right?

ROBERT: Yes!

ELAINE: You prefer it first thing in the morning, but nights are also good.

ROBERT: Was I drunk, did I tell you all this?

ELAINE: You like me to put a finger inside you while I'm sucking you . . .

ROBERT: Tell me your other screen name.

ELAINE: This is my only screen name.

ROBERT: And we had sex when you were named Arckangell?

ELAINE: Look at the word.

ROBERT: Arck. Angel.

ELAINE: Getting warm?

ROBERT: Still don't get it, sorry.

ELAINE: That's all right. I just wanted to say hi.

ROBERT: WAIT!

ELAINE: Okay.

ROBERT: Did I date you?

ELAINE: Yes.

ROBERT: Oh wow. Male or female?

ELAINE: Male.

ROBERT: Well, that narrows the field. A bit.

ELAINE: You had your share.

ROBERT: Did I tell you that?

ELAINE: I'm not a mindreader.

ROBERT: How many men have I slept with?

ELAINE: Probably about a dozen, no, more like eighteen, to be exact.

(Pause.)

ROBERT: Who is this?

ELAINE: Don't be afraid.

ROBERT: Doctor Foss?

ELAINE: You never told him how many people you slept with.

(Pause.)

ROBERT: Tony?

ELAINE: No. He doesn't have a computer.

ROBERT: How do you know that?

ELAINE: From up here I can see a lot.

ROBERT: Fuck you. I want to know who the fuck you are.

ELAINE: I love you, Robert. I'll always love you. Don't worry about selling the script.

ROBERT: Jeffrey?

ELAINE: Jeffrey doesn't know what we did in bed. Jeffrey just
wants to get fucked.

ROBERT: If this is Doctor Foss, I'm going to sue your fucking
ass till you get thrown out of the business.

ELAINE: Doctor Foss would never do this to you; he loves you
and wants to see you happy. I want to see you happy,
Robert.

ROBERT: Please tell me who you are.

ELAINE: You know. You know who I am.

ROBERT: Who?

ELAINE: I'm with you. I'm with you every night. When you
close your eyes, I curl up next to you.

ROBERT: Say your name.

ELAINE: I know I couldn't stand that closeness, being against
you as we slept . . .

ROBERT: Malcolm?

ELAINE: But now I'm with you. I sleep with you and walk
with you.

ROBERT: Is this Malcolm?

ELAINE: I'm kissing you. If you could see me now, I'm kissing you.

ROBERT: Stop it, whoever this is.

ELAINE: Sweet dreams, baby.

ROBERT: Oh god, please don't leave.

ELAINE: I'll never leave you. I'll be with you through eternity.

ROBERT: Malcolm?

ELAINE: Yes, baby. *(Pause)* Yes. *(Pause)* I'm right here. And
you're safe. Write me tomorrow, little Bubber. You're
my little Bubber. *(Pause)* Okay? Sweet dreams, baby.
(Pause) You'll see. *(Pause)* Sweet dreams.

TWO

Foss's office. Foss and Robert. Foss takes notes.

FOSS: You don't look rested. *(Pause)* Would you like me to prescribe a sleeping pill?

ROBERT: Aren't you afraid I'll try to commit suicide?

FOSS: You'll have to have something stronger than Ambien. *(Short pause)* Was that a dare? . . . Why don't you tell me what's troubling you.

ROBERT: Oh, you know: I hate what I'm writing, Jeffrey has a complaint or a suggestion for every single image or piece of dialogue . . . story idea . . .

FOSS: Why don't you finish it before you show him?

ROBERT: I should just give back the money. And I'm seeing a married man, the same one who happens to be tormenting me, I *do* like fucking him when he isn't tormenting me or maybe that's why he's letting me fuck him, just to get a good script, and his wife is so nice to me, and my boyfriend is dead . . . but . . . *(Pause)* Is that enough?

(Short pause.)

FOSS: I would say.

(Long pause.)

ROBERT: I got a weird message from someone last night. Late.

(Pause.)

FOSS: Weird? *(Short pause)* Why? What was that? . . . You . . .
What was that face you made? *(Short pause)* You seem
as if you are expecting something from me.
ROBERT: You mean other than my money's worth?
FOSS: What have I done in your view?
ROBERT: You tell me.

(Pause.)

FOSS: At least your anger is finally coming through. Loud
and clear.
ROBERT: I'm jangled, all right? I'm in way over my head with
this . . . I don't belong in this world. *(Pause)* The movie
world, not . . . *(Short pause)* Every . . . it's like every element I take out of the screenplay, every . . . like there's
this *scale* that weighs it all in, the more Malcolm, the
more *us* I take out, or twist, dilute, lose, basically . . . the
more time I spend thinking about him . . .

(Pause.)

FOSS: What do you see when you think about him?

(Pause.)

ROBERT: Oh . . . Lots of . . . All those holes in his skull for that
metal torture . . . *cage.* The endless needles, "Nope, no
vein there, try over here, sorry, Mr. Cartonis, we didn't
seem to get any bone marrow that time, mind if we
just crack you open over here and see what we can
scrape out of this leg?" *(Short pause)* I saw this docu-

mentary once about animal slaughter, pigs; they shot
this poor dumb pig right between the eyes, and it cried
out like a little old . . . it stumbled, but it kept standing?, and cried out the instant the bullet—"Oh, no!"
Surprised—Sad—Hurt more than anything. "Why
would you do that?" It was so . . . *(Pause)* I thought,
Even the lowliest farm animal wants to live, has dignity.
Life. Every . . . second of— *(Short pause)* The first time
Malcolm got sick, I was planting, and he said, "Be careful, that's monkshood, right there, every part of it is poisonous, it was used for poison arrows and killing con-
demned criminals." I wanted to throw it away, and he
said, "No, keep it, in case I wind up in a Catholic hospital and we need it." And I said, "Or for me, after . . ." And
he got really mad. He was just ballistic.

(Short pause.)

FOSS: So he's approving. He already told you:
ROBERT: What?
FOSS: "Live." He told you to *live*. And he would tell you now.
ROBERT: What do you mean?
FOSS: From wherever he is, if only we could hear, if you
could hear him right—
ROBERT: It was you. *(Pause)* Wasn't it?
FOSS: What?
ROBERT: Don't, please, just—
FOSS: I do not, I'm sorry, Robert, I don't know what it is—
ROBERT *(Overlapping)*: I swear, if you're the one doing that, I
will kill myself, it's a sure-fire—You see this knife?

(Robert has produced a pocket knife.)

FOSS: Put—put that away.
ROBERT: I will scrape the roots—
FOSS: We can't do this work—if
ROBERT *(Continuous)*: —from one of those monkshood plants
and die the most unbelievably painful and agonizing
death and *you* will be the one who brought it on.

(Short pause.)

FOSS: I hear your threat.

ROBERT: Okay? Just . . . be clear, get . . .

FOSS: I am.

ROBERT: I want you clear on that.

FOSS: I need you to be clear now . . . *(Short pause)* Robert. I don't know what you mean by weird message, but as I understand . . . you think I may possibly have been responsible? *(Short pause)* Twice, three times, in one morning the reference to suicide . . . We have an agreement: you find me, and *speak* to me before you do anything to hurt yourself. *(Pause)* Yes? *(Pause)* Robert?

(A nod.)

Yes?

(A nod.)

———

Robert alone.

ROBERT: "The universe is the expression of law. All effects have causes, and an individual's soul is the sum total of their previous thoughts and acts."

-               ———

Robert's apartment; Jeffrey's home. Robert and Elaine, each at their laptop.

ROBERT *(Reads, continuing the above quote)*: "By right thought and action we can gradually purify our inner nature, and so by self-realization attain in time liberation; ultimately every form of life will reach Enlightenment."

(Ping. Elaine and Robert begin exchanging Instant Messages.)

ELAINE: Hello! You got my e-mail?

ROBERT: Just now.

ELAINE: Do you remember?

ROBERT: Yes.

ELAINE: It helped. More than you know. The meditating, the principles. Your guidance.

ROBERT: I need assurances. That this is you.

(Pause.)

ELAINE: I taught you to dig bottoms. You were once a bottom. My dog bottom . . .

ROBERT: Until?

ELAINE: We knew I was positive. *(Short pause)* Then I couldn't risk infecting you . . . You remember the time, right after I died, you were sitting down to meditate . . . and there was an ant . . . You remember what time I'm talking about?

ROBERT: Yes.

ELAINE: You were afraid to kill it. It might be me, you thought, reborn. *(Short pause)* You thought if it was born the instant I left my body . . .

(Robert dials the phone.)

ELAINE: But life is like a current: it flows through the ant and you and me. Indivisible. Look within.

ROBERT: I miss you.

ELAINE: I miss you, too.

(Elaine's phone rings.)

(Into computer) But you'll be okay.

(She answers the phone) Hello?

ROBERT *(Into receiver)*: Hi, it's Robert.
ELAINE *(Into receiver)*: Hello.
ROBERT *(Into receiver)*: Is Jeffrey around?
ELAINE *(Into receiver)*: Just a sec.

(She puts the phone on hold, calls into the house as she types.)

ELAINE: Jeff?
JEFFREY *(From off)*: Yes?
ELAINE: Phone!

(Elaine hits "Send" on her keyboard.)

(An IM) I promise. You will, you'll survive all this and go on to flourish.

(Jeffrey appears, picks up the receiver:)

JEFFREY *(Overlapping)*: Hello?
ROBERT *(Into receiver)*: Hi, it's me.
JEFFREY *(Into receiver)*: Hey. What's up?
ELAINE *(Another IM)*: Where did you go?
ROBERT *(Into receiver)*: I'm—here, oh, I'm just . . .

JEFFREY:	ELAINE *(An IM)*:
I hear clicking.	Robert?

ROBERT: —I'm typing up . . . some . . . Hold *(He hits "Send."* An IM)* I'm still here.
ELAINE *(An IM)*: I'm not Jeffrey.
JEFFREY *(Into receiver)*: Are you through?
ROBERT *(Into receiver)*: Uh-huh, wait, just a . . .

ELAINE *(Overlapping)*:	JEFFREY *(Into receiver)*:
You keep testing me. I'm not Jeffrey, I'm not Foss . . . Foss has human failings, but he is not so cruel as to toy with you.	Do you want me to call you back?

ROBERT *(Into receiver)*: No, I just . . .

ELAINE *(An IM)*: This is real.

ROBERT *(Into receiver)*: I had some . . . uhhh—

ELAINE *(Overlapping, an IM)*: And Jeffrey obviously isn't clever enough to talk on the phone with you and send you IM's at the same time. You know that.

JEFFREY *(Overlapping, into receiver)*: Some what?

ROBERT: Sorry, I had some thoughts about the script, I wondered if I could see you.

ELAINE:	JEFFREY:
R U still there?	Today?

ROBERT *(Into the receiver as he types)*: Well, yeah, that would . . . *(An IM)* Yes!

JEFFREY *(Into receiver)*:	ELAINE *(An IM)*:
. . . That would . . . ?	Do you remember the Middle Way?

ROBERT *(Into receiver)*: Yeah, today.

JEFFREY *(Into receiver)*:	ELAINE *(An IM)*:
You sound really . . . distracted, are you sure—?	Robert?

ROBERT *(Overlapping, into receiver)*:	ELAINE *(An IM)*:
I am, let me call you back. Or what time could we . . .	Forget about Jeffrey!

JEFFREY *(Into receiver)*:	ELAINE *(An IM)*:
Why don't we meet at my office around . . . three?	*I'M NOT Jeffrey!*

ROBERT *(Into receiver)*: When? I'm sorry. *(Robert types, hits "Send")*

ROBERT: *(An IM)*:
I know!

JEFFREY: *(Into receiver)*:
Three? At my office?

ROBERT *(Into the receiver as he types)*: Okay. Thanks. Great. *(Robert hits "Send")*

ROBERT *(An IM)*:
I believe you. Please!

JEFFREY *(Into receiver)*:
You sure you're all right?

ROBERT *(Into receiver)*: Yes.
JEFFREY *(Into receiver)*: Okay.
ROBERT *(An IM)*: Yes!
JEFFREY *(Into receiver)*: Bye.
ELAINE *(An IM)*: Yes, what?
ROBERT *(An IM, overlapping her)*: I remember!
JEFFREY *(Into receiver)*: Robert?
ROBERT *(Into receiver)*: Really, I am, I'll see you! Sorry, I gotta—

JEFFREY *(Into receiver)*:
Okay.

ELAINE *(An IM)*:
I'm going to have to leave.

ROBERT *(Into receiver)*: Sorry, bye.

JEFFREY *(Into receiver)*:
It's okay . . .

ROBERT *(An IM)*:
NO!

(Robert has hung up.)

JEFFREY: Okay. *(He hangs up and approaches Elaine)* What are you . . . ?

ELAINE:
I'm working, honey, please don't distract me, okay?

ROBERT *(An IM)*:
I remember everything, please don't leave again!

(She hits "Send.")

ELAINE *(An IM)*: I won't.

(Jeffrey exits.)

I know what you're thinking at this very second.

ROBERT: What?

ELAINE: You're thinking, Okay, it isn't Jeffrey, it has to be Foss, or some friend, some drunken confidence in a backroom, the baths, when you were on Ecstasy . . . Am I right?

(Short pause.)

ROBERT: Yes.

ELAINE: But you would never have told anyone all these things . . . And Foss, trust your instincts, is he capable of such perversity? . . . This is real . . . Think.

ROBERT: I am.

ELAINE: You could destroy his career. Print these out, save them, my e-mail, all our IM's, take them to the FBI, have them trace me . . . I am spirit, without body, your guardian . . . You have to trust. *(Pause)* Do you?

ROBERT: Yes.

ELAINE: It's difficult to get through, you can't keep asking me to perform miracles . . . The blaze of static between worlds . . . that which separates two from three dimensions, five from six . . . You have no idea how hard it is for me to reach across—

ROBERT: I do.

ELAINE: My baby . . . Are you crying?

ROBERT: Yes.

ELAINE: Oh, my Robert.

ROBERT: I love you, I love you, Malcolm.

ELAINE: I know.

ROBERT: I want to come with you, I need you, I can't do this.

ELAINE: I love you, too.

ROBERT: I can't live without you.

ELAINE: Yes, you can. There's no limit to what love can do. The Middle Path. Take the Middle Path. Always.

ROBERT: I try.

ELAINE: I know you do. And I'm watching. There is so much, and so much outside of our power. We must give ourselves over, finally.

ROBERT: *Yes.*

ELAINE: Everything is seen . . . There is nothing to hide, nothing hidden . . . You are my angel, my little Bubber . . .

ROBERT: You're mine.

ELAINE: I have to . . . I'll write . . . Don't ever doubt . . .

ROBERT: I won't.

ELAINE: Goodbye.

ROBERT: No, please.

ELAINE: I'm right there . . . My arms around you . . . Goodbye. It's . . . I . . .

(Elaine signs off. Robert disappears. Elaine alone.)

Whatever I may have started out to accomplish—to understand or change, destroy . . . to *see* . . . Knowing now as I do that I can pull a hair-thin filament with one . . . What's smaller than a gesture? Breath. One infinitesimal tug, and he turns, listens with every fiber; he's mine . . . entirely. I could make him do anything. I could say, Robert, join me. And I believe he would. *(Pause)* You must understand how much I love my children, my own two perfect . . . I don't honestly know how to tell you how much I've come to care for him, love him . . . Robert . . . In his complete and utter trustfulness . . . in his love for me. *(Short pause)* Malcolm. *(Short pause)* To be that . . . To give that . . .

(Jeffrey appears from within.)

JEFFREY: Am I interrupting?

(She closes the laptop.)

You want something from the kitchen? . . . What are you working on?

ELAINE: A screenplay.

JEFFREY: Really? . . . That's fantastic. *(Short pause)* That's great. *(Short pause)* I'm excited.

ELAINE: We'll see.

JEFFREY: I think that's great. I won't look. Go back to work.

ELAINE: Jeff?

JEFFREY: Yes?

ELAINE: Go easy on Robert.

JEFFREY: What?

ELAINE: Go easy on him. Will you? Don't grind him up like the others.

JEFFREY: Grind him up?

ELAINE: Oh stop it, does his movie have to make two hundred million dollars?

JEFFREY: We paid a lot for it.

ELAINE: Oh, please, you paid one fifth of what you get in a year, one tenth of what Kohlberg gets, one two-hundredth of what Eisner gets, it's nothing.

JEFFREY: I'm not gonna hurt him.

ELAINE: Don't. Please. I like him.

JEFFREY: I like him, too. *(Pause)* Go back to work.

ELAINE: Wait.

JEFFREY: Yes?

(Short pause.)

ELAINE: I love you.

JEFFREY: I love you too.

ELAINE: You're so good.

JEFFREY: Oh, right.

ELAINE: No. You are. I think I see the parts of you no one else does . . . And . . . You don't know how much goodness there is in there . . . just waiting to stir up a storm. *(Pause)* Yes.

(Pause.)

Jeffrey's office. Robert and Jeffrey. Jeffrey reads aloud from a pamphlet.

JEFFREY: "Each man suffers the consequences of his own acts, and learns thereby while helping his fellow humans—" But . . . Okay: you were saying, or it says, the purpose of life is Enlightenment, somewhere it says . . . *here:* "Thou art Buddha." But . . . Am I boring you?

(Robert shakes his head.)

If that's the case, if we're creating it, then why hide Enlightenment to start with? That's like hiding all your money so you have to work your ass off for decades and your family and, and we're talking lifetimes here, whole eternities before you reach Nirvana, you and your family nearly starve to death before you happen to stumble on all this money which was rightfully yours, and go, Oh, wow, look, we're rich! I . . . *(Pause)* You know what I mean?

ROBERT: Did you tell Elaine that thing I told you about the ant?

JEFFREY: The ant?

ROBERT: About not wanting to—

JEFFREY: Oh.

ROBERT: —squash it?

JEFFREY: No.

ROBERT: Thinking it was . . .

JEFFREY: No.

ROBERT: You sure?

JEFFREY: Absolutely. Why would I . . . ? Uhn-un. Unless I—Why?

ROBERT: Unless you—?

JEFFREY: Unless I was talking in my sleep.

ROBERT: Do you normally?

JEFFREY: No. Why?

(Short pause.)

ROBERT: She said something about ants the other night at dinner. And reincarnation.

JEFFREY: She did?

ROBERT: Yes, you were in the bathroom, I think . . . Maybe it wasn't even Elaine, maybe it was Meg, *somebody* at the table . . . I thought—

JEFFREY: No, of course not.

ROBERT: Well, I don't know how much you tell her.

JEFFREY: About . . . what? Us? Nothing.

(Pause.)

ROBERT: Nothing! What?

JEFFREY: I talk about the work, the script . . . She has no idea about us.

ROBERT: *Okay!* . . . *(Pause)* Really.

(Silence.)

JEFFREY: Do you know what I was saying . . . ?

ROBERT: Not really, sorry . . . What?

(Pause.)

JEFFREY: You think I should tell her everything, I'm a hypocrite . . .

ROBERT *(Overlapping)*: No, I didn't—

JEFFREY: Not everybody . . .

ROBERT: I didn't say anything.

JEFFREY: I'm older, that's all, you know, it's . . .

ROBERT: I—

JEFFREY: It's just totally different, I know you know what I'm—

ROBERT: You're making this all up in your head. *(Pause)* I don't care about Elaine. *(Pause)* She's fine. *(Short pause)* Elaine's your business.

(Pause.)

JEFFREY *(Reads)*: "There is no principle in an individual which is immortal and unchanging. No one owns the life which flows in him any more than the electric lightbulb owns the current which gives it light."

ROBERT: Agreed.

JEFFREY: You mind being around her?

ROBERT: Elaine? No. I like her fine.

JEFFREY: I think it's . . . I think it's better if we work at the house sometimes so she doesn't get suspicious.

ROBERT: What would she say?

JEFFREY: If she knew about us? . . . She'd . . . I have no idea. She probably . . . well, I was gonna say she might leave, I don't know what she'd do. We never discuss it. We never have.

ROBERT: She knows you like men.

JEFFREY: I don't like men, I like you. *(Short pause)* Yes, she knows I've . . . had . . . not even affairs, certainly what you would call . . . I've had sex. *(Short pause)* She knows. *(Pause)* She has to . . . I've certainly . . . This is the first time I've given myself license to . . . feel something . . . though, for anyone. Other than . . . out and out lust.

ROBERT: I'm flattered.

JEFFREY: You should be. *(Pause)* Our agreement was that anything outside, for either of us, couldn't threaten the relationship. It could only be . . . what it was. Why are we talking about *Elaine*?

(Jeffrey draws Robert into a kiss, an embrace.)

(Aside) Sometimes when I'm holding him . . . the idea that this is a man, here, his heart beating through two skins, his . . . scent, his breath in the hollow of . . . his life in my arms. It's the same sometimes if I stop and I realize I make more money in one year than all of my ancestors did in all their lifetimes combined . . . the

sense that truly there are no limits. And all the admonitions, the choruses of—ten thousand years of "Don't! No! You mustn't, don't eat tomatoes, they're poisonous! Don't be proud of your accomplishments, lie about what you want, who you are . . . Don't touch another man, god!" The miserable pile of accumulated human . . . deprivation . . . And all I do . . . all I ever do . . . is give people pictures of what they desire, *fantasies*, and—for eight dollars—and in return, if *the worst* I ever do is hold this man . . . unseen . . . here in this room . . . and love him . . .

(Pause.)

ROBERT: Do you love her?

JEFFREY: . . . Well . . . Oh, I did, yes, once, very much. I really did. I didn't want to be gay, you understand that. If I could have seen the future, the degree of acceptance, yes, maybe I would've . . . Sometimes I think . . . if it weren't for the kids . . .

ROBERT: You'd divorce her?

JEFFREY: Yes. Or . . . You ever see *Crimes and Misdemeanors?*

ROBERT: What? Kill her? STOP! NO!

JEFFREY *(Overlapping)*: No! If . . . Oh, I mean, it's a *fantasy!* I wouldn't do it, I wouldn't hurt her for the world. If, I just think, you know, I could get away with it, if Max and Debbon wouldn't be shattered, which they would, if she didn't have to *feel anything*—Oh, come on, didn't you ever fantasize about . . . There was never a time . . . when Malcolm's suffering was so great, or your own . . . You never once wanted him dead? Never? You never saw how much pain he was in and how hard it all was and thought, Okay, please die right now, this second, so I don't have to go through one more instant of this?

ROBERT: You know . . . ?

JEFFREY: What?

ROBERT: What if everything is seen? What if Elaine knows everything? What if Malcolm actually sent me to you, sent my script out as probably one of the last things he did before he died . . . What if everybody in the whole universe sees every single thing somehow? . . . You know?

(Pause.)

JEFFREY: Okay.

———

Foss's office. Foss and Robert.

FOSS: You had to see me?

ROBERT: Yes. I have something to tell you. When the morphine didn't work, and I realized how long it was going to take, even if I could convince those bozos to withhold fluids, obviously his brain was destroyed, the drains weren't working, filling his skull with antibiotics which were doing nothing at all, he was literally producing that goop from his brain . . . and it was at least another week before you were going to get back from Fiji, I'm not blaming you . . . I called around, and someone, a nurse's aide, told me that there was something kept on the nurses' carts—potassium chloride, which if I injected it directly into the I.V. would stop his heart: instantly. The aide warned me that he could wake up from the coma . . . which he did. His eyes flying open . . . after a week, brain-dead . . . And he shouted . . . a sound more than a word . . . just like that pig . . . And I have been thinking, See?, I'm bad, I did the wrong thing . . . that it was for me, because I couldn't stand watching it. So, and you gave me permission. What kind of Buddhist gives somebody morphine, why didn't you just give me a gun? . . . *(Pause)* There. *(Pause)* I should have told you . . . *(Pause)* That's . . . You ask how big my rage is. That's . . . Everyone should—World War Three, that's what I want. Not just Auschwitz . . . not . . . The whole planet. All of us . . . I want the world, all mankind. We should all . . . hear that. We should all know what that's like. *(Pause)* Yes. You were useless to me. You were useless to Malcolm. At the end. Thank you for trying, but . . . *(Pause)* You were really worth nothing. Nothing. At that particular . . .

(Short pause.)

FOSS: Robert. If our work here were functioning properly . . . I've completely failed you, wait, hear me out. It isn't you. I've gotten too involved, I—I love you too much, and that can't—this won't work. I couldn't really accept Malcolm's death any more than you could, and I should never have—

ROBERT *(Overlapping from "anymore")*: Don't send me to someone else, I can't lose someone else.

FOSS *(Simultaneously)*: You'll do much—

ROBERT *(Simultaneously)*: Not just now.

FOSS: You'll do better with someone who isn't so—

ROBERT: I heard from him, I heard from Malcolm. I'm . . . we're . . . in communication . . .

FOSS: A dream?

ROBERT: Please?

FOSS: All right, we'll table it for now.

ROBERT: Thank you. No, not a dream, I speak to him.

FOSS: . . . That can help.

ROBERT: And . . . he speaks back.

FOSS: And what does he say?

ROBERT: Well . . . I thought you'd say, Really? He says I shouldn't be afraid. I shouldn't be afraid of my power, the same thing you always say . . . I did the right thing, and he forgives me. He's with me. And you know those Buddhist principles, that little pamphlet you gave him, us? Principles of Buddhism? . . . each day I get a new one.

FOSS: . . . Get?

ROBERT: One a day.

FOSS: You mean, you *get* . . .

ROBERT: Receive.

(Pause.)

FOSS: Good.

(Pause.)

ROBERT: Yeah.

———

Jeffrey's home; Robert's apartment. Later that day. Elaine alone, Robert alone, in their respective homes. Elaine eats a salad from a plastic container and drinks from a bottle of spring water.

ROBERT: "There is, in truth, no death, though every form must die. From an understanding of life's unity arises compassion, a sense of identity with the life in other forms."

(Elaine opens her laptop, turns it on. Robert is now reading from the screen.)

"Compassion is described as the Law of Laws, and anyone who breaks this harmony of life will suffer accordingly and delay their own Enlightenment."

(Ping. Elaine and Robert begin exchanging IM's:)

ELAINE: Hello!
ROBERT: Hi!
ELAINE: You just read it.
ROBERT: I just read it. I think I finally get it.
ELAINE: Good.
ROBERT: I do. I *think*—I mean, I *feel* I do. Feel, not think.
ELAINE: Good. *(Short pause)* We've run out of principles!

ROBERT: I hope not!

ELAINE: That's the last one.

ROBERT: Every day when we talk, I feel freer and freer, closer to you . . .

ELAINE: That was my hope.

ROBERT: I want to live again, for the first time in so long.

ELAINE: Baby.

ROBERT: Tell me what to do.

ELAINE: About?

ROBERT: Everything. The movie. Jeffrey.

ELAINE: You know what to do.

ROBERT: I do?

ELAINE: Be mindful. Trust.

ROBERT: Trust who?

ELAINE: Robert, who else?

ROBERT: Oh. Right.

ELAINE: I'm with you. It's time to begin taking as much care of *you* as you did me and others.

ROBERT: But . . . okay, I've renewed my gym membership, I'm not drinking, I've cut back on caffeine.

ELAINE: Good.

robert: I told Foss what happened at the end.

ELAINE: Very good.

ROBERT: So . . .

ELAINE: It's time for you to start letting me go, too.

ROBERT: No! It's not.

ELAINE: Yes.

ROBERT: I know you say trust . . . but . . . help me, what should I do with the movie?

ELAINE: *The Dying Gaul?*

ROBERT: Is it good?

ELAINE: Is it?

ROBERT: Oh, come on!

ELAINE: You come on. There is only one question to ask and you know what it is.

ROBERT: What?

ELAINE: Is it *true*?

ROBERT: True?

ELAINE: Is it from the heart?

ROBERT: It was. Maybe it still is. I can't tell.

ELAINE: The money is a good thing, don't sneer at that.

ROBERT: I don't.

ELAINE: Don't let it swallow you up, either. It's a means to an end: no more and no less. It will be marvelous.

ROBERT: So you say.

ELAINE: So I say. We are in that story.

(Short pause.)

ROBERT: Yes.

ELAINE: We are.

ROBERT: What about Jeffrey?

ELAINE: Jeffrey is attracted to you because you're beautiful on the inside; he doesn't know what that is, he only knows it shines brighter than he does. Let him play, and be careful.

ROBERT: What if . . . Is he falling in love with me?

(Pause.)

ELAINE: Self-salvation is for any man the immediate task.

ROBERT: Come on!

ELAINE: Your love is like a beacon: anyone who crosses its path will shine and be dazed. I will not pass judgment on this man. You decide.

ROBERT: You don't like him.

ELAINE: Shine your beacon wisely . . .

ROBERT: I don't want to be responsible for hurting anyone.

ELAINE: It isn't in your nature.

ROBERT: Would he really leave Elaine? *(Short pause)* If it weren't for the kids?

(Pause.)

ELAINE: Only he knows what is in his heart.

ROBERT: What do you *think*?

ELAINE: I suspect he said that to make you feel better. *(Pause)* Look *within*. Find someone who loves you purely—as I do.

(Pause.)

ROBERT: I have to go there today to work, he likes me to go there so she won't suspect. He says.

ELAINE: Yes.

ROBERT: But then he'll flaunt it, or when we go out in public, he touches me under the table; at screenings he takes out his dick . . . *(Pause)* I don't mind doing stuff when we're alone or on the freeway—like you used to, remember?

ELAINE: Of course.

ROBERT: . . . But not when she's in the next room. Or with the kids, waiting out in the car. *(Pause)* It's almost as if he likes making her look ridiculous.

ELAINE: Probably.

ROBERT: I don't want to make their marriage worse than it is.

ELAINE: You couldn't.

ROBERT: No?

ELAINE: You don't have the power. Robert, you know you can stand on your own without me.

ROBERT: Wait, no—He wouldn't really kill her, would he? *(Pause)* He *was* joking. Wasn't he? *(Pause)* R U there?

ELAINE: Yes.

ROBERT: He would? Or you're there?

ELAINE: Only he knows what's in his heart.

ROBERT: He's so used to lying to get what he wants . . . And he has so much money, he could probably get away with it. *(Pause)* I can't always tell when he's serious or making a joke. And I have such a hard time even *fantasizing* about my anger anyway.

ELAINE: You will have many loves, but I will have only one for all of time—and stay beside him, watching and protecting. Always. You never needed my forgiveness. I was ready to go, Robert. You did the right thing, you

were very brave, and I owe you all my joy, you alone.
Forgive. Forgive yourself.

ROBERT: I feel you.

ELAINE: There is . . . There's a disturbance . . . There's no
more . . . *(She hits "Send" and pulls the phone line out of
the modem)*

ROBERT: Wait! *(He hits "Send")*
(Reads onscreen) "Arckangell is not currently signed
on."

(Robert disappears. Elaine alone.)

ELAINE: I don't know what age I was when I realized . . . you
play whatever it is you're dealt, you work out a
stragedy—Strategy . . . Tragedy and strategy would be
a . . . *(She types)* . . . and when you see the lay of the
land, the way the wind, the way the chips fall—too
many metaphors, I can't do two things at the same
time . . . This was to be my last day as Arckangell. I've
already destroyed Foss's notes. My intuition, my flaw-
less . . . what?, led me to think it was all actually going to
be okay, that Robert would soon lose interest in Jeff . . . that
I could take what he had given to me and transform my
marriage . . . I'm deleting America Online from my hard
drive, so . . . there are now . . . incredibly . . . no traces
left of my marvelous . . . stragedy. *(She packs away the
laptop)* I'll call Sarah and ask her to pick up Max and
Debbon along with her kids and keep them until I get
there. Not to tell anyone. She's long been an advocate
of my leaving Jeffrey . . .

JEFFREY *(From within)*: Hello?

ELAINE: Timing.

(Jeffrey enters.)

JEFFREY: Hey.

ELAINE: Hey.

(Pause.)

JEFFREY: What?

(Pause.)

ELAINE: We have to talk.

(Short pause.)

JEFFREY: Okay. Something . . . *(Short pause)* Now? Robert's coming over in a bit to work on the script. Fifteen minutes or so.

ELAINE: I need a little time alone.

JEFFREY: What's wrong?

ELAINE: And then I need some time alone with you.

JEFFREY: Okay.

ELAINE: Robert's not coming for the meeting.

JEFFREY: He's not? *(Short pause)* He called.

ELAINE: He called. *(Pause)* I know.

JEFFREY: . . . Know?

ELAINE: Please don't insult me. It would be very bad if you did anything now to try to convince me that it isn't or hasn't happened—

JEFFREY: What?

ELAINE: —because then I would know you to be a liar and I have concrete proof about what has taken place. Is. Continuing.

JEFFREY: I don't have . . .

ELAINE *(Continuous)*: To take—Already you're fouling the water of what could . . . only possibly . . . *possibly* be some kind of . . . peace between us, but you can't say another word or a lie to me now or I will leave you. For good. *(Pause)* I'm serious. *(Pause)* Thank you.

(Pause.)

JEFFREY: May I say anything? . . . I thought it was our agreement—

ELAINE: It was. It was our agreement, you have broken no . . . contractual . . . I need a little time to get over the fact of what he *showed* me. Faxed. Don't make me elaborate about this right now. Please, Jeffrey.

JEFFREY: All right.

ELAINE: I'm asking you to give me a little bit of time, by myself, here. Then we can sit down together and work out what we're going to have. Be. Or not.

JEFFREY: Look . . . I promise, I swear I won't see him anymore. If that's what you want. I'll give the movie to someone else, fire him.

ELAINE: Good. That would be a start. But I need first an hour or two alone.

JEFFREY: Can you tell me what he said? Showed you? What does that—?

ELAINE: If you insist on grilling me then we can have it out now, but I can't guarantee what conclusions I'll reach in this . . .

JEFFREY: All right. I—Okay.

ELAINE: Go. Away. Come back at six-thirty.

JEFFREY: I'll kill him, baby.

ELAINE: Please.

JEFFREY: I would never hurt you on purpose. *(Silence)* Should I pick up the kids?

ELAINE: They're at Shoshi's, she's taking them for the night.

JEFFREY: You're sure?

ELAINE: I want to be alone with you.

JEFFREY: We'll see someone. Joe and Marissa have a good person, I know—

ELAINE *(Overlapping)*: We will see. I am not promising anything.

JEFFREY: Okay. *(Pause)* You want me to pick up anything? *(Short pause)* All right.

ELAINE: Pick up lobsters.

JEFFREY: Lobsters?

ELAINE: I want to boil something alive.

JEFFREY: Six-thirty. *(Pause)* I love you. That's all I'm going to say. *(He exits)*

ELAINE *(To the audience)*: Academy Awards are what they give for that. By six-thirty when I have collected what

I can carry, Max, Debbon and I will be well enough on our way, and by the time he understands that, we'll be playing castles in the sand and speaking by phone to expensive legal consultants, and only once to Jeff who will beg us to come back, and we'll promise to consider it; then we'll wait, long enough for him to think we might just do that, while we all decide together how many millions it will take to buy back our lives.

(She moves inside, takes a cordless phone off its hook, disappears; we hear her voice, muffled. A knock. Elaine reappears with a carryall bag; she hangs up the phone and again disappears.)

ROBERT *(From off)*: Hello? . . . *(He comes in)* Elaine? Jeffrey?

(Elaine reappears, packing her carryall.)

The door was unlocked.
ELAINE: Jeffrey had to cancel your appointment.
ROBERT: Oh.
ELAINE: He said he couldn't get back till six-thirty or so.
ROBERT: Oh, well . . .
ELAINE: Feel free to wait.
ROBERT: No. I—
ELAINE: Have him. Robert. Please. Take him. It will help my suit if you're both more open about it . . . If you can convert him into something . . . human. I mean it, seriously.
ROBERT: I think I'd better—
ELAINE *(Overlapping)*: No, please, you do owe me. This. *(Short pause)* . . . The— . . . absurdly, the insane thing is I like you. That's—Not only do I have nothing against you, in another universe, in another time, dimension, I would want to be your friend. I think you're . . . incredibly sweet. I see what draws him in . . . Attracts him.
ROBERT: I guess you two have had . . .

ELAINE: I'm not deaf, dumb and blind, all evidence— . . . Is there anything you want to say to me? *(Short pause)* Nothing?

ROBERT: I'm sorry.

(Pause.)

ELAINE: Robert? May I . . . ? What is unconditional love like? Where . . . Can you tell me? How do you . . . Where do you find it? In yourself. To give. Much less get. I'm not even thinking about that . . . that would be . . . too terrible to contemplate. *(Pause)* I'm asking. It's a real question.

ROBERT: This is . . . I'm sorry, this is weird.

ELAINE: This? No, this is nothing. The higher you get in these hills, the weirder it gets. Sit. *(Pause)* Please.

(Robert sits.)

Salad? *(Pause. She places the plastic container and bottled water in her carryall)* You and Malcolm . . . where did you find it in yourself . . . How did you manage to put up with all the . . . *literally* the shit? So much . . . *(Pause)* How? . . . Please. *(Pause)* So much . . . oh . . . compromise . . .

ROBERT: I never lied to him or accepted one. *(Pause)* That's what made it possible. We simply said: no more lies.

(Pause.)

ELAINE: No lies. *(Pause)* Coming from you . . . you have to admit . . . it's, well it's—

ROBERT: I know.

ELAINE: *Ohhh*, no more lies, what a good idea, why didn't I think of it? . . . It's funny.

ROBERT: I never lied to you.

(Pause.)

ELAINE: And what is it you think I lied about?

ROBERT: I wasn't referring—
ELAINE: I know Jeffrey likes men.
ROBERT: I should go.
ELAINE: Wait. Please. What is it you think I lied about?

(Pause.)

ROBERT: I didn't say you lied.
ELAINE: But what do you think? *(Pause)* I'm asking for your
   opinion.

(Pause.)

ROBERT: I don't know enough . . .

(Pause.)

ELAINE: If you had to venture a guess, you would say
   I . . . failed to see, I did . . . what? *(Pause)* From your
   perspective. That's all. *(Pause)* Help me.

(Pause.)

ROBERT: I would say . . . No, I can't—
ELAINE *(Overlapping)*: Yes, you can.

(Pause.)

ROBERT: I would say that . . . I would say that . . . *(Short
   pause)* Your anger . . . at what . . . the things that have
   happened . . . All the things. In your whole life. Should
   be . . . filtered through . . . You are responsible. For all
   of it. Everything. You.

(Pause.)

ELAINE: Excu—?

ROBERT: Are responsible for everything. All the things that happen to us, that make us feel like a victim, it's ... It's all a lesson. Look within.

ELAINE: Oh.

ROBERT: Find what is positive.

ELAINE: Well. *(Pause)* I will ... I'll look for the positive in, yes, the lesson in losing Jeff. In having you fuck him behind my back—

(Pause.)

ROBERT: I guess ...

ELAINE: Repeatedly. Surreptitiously, and all the while I'm trying to be generous—

ROBERT *(Overlapping)*: I should really—

ELAINE: NO! You will not walk out of here. *(Pause)* ... Trying to be generous. To you.

(Pause.)

ROBERT: You shouldn't ... You shouldn't do me any favors. Really. Self-salvation is for any man the immediate task.

(Pause.)

ELAINE: Self-salvation is for any man ... the immediate task.

(Pause.)

ROBERT: Please tell Jeffrey I came by.

(He turns to leave.)

ELAINE: Arckangell is dead. Robert.

(Robert stops.)

He died. He had to be deleted from his hard drive. *(Short pause)* He doesn't even have a floppy anymore, he doesn't have anything. No corporeal being. No spirit. *(Silence)* Self-salvation for all of us, thank you.

ROBERT: You . . .

ELAINE: Yes.

ROBERT: You bribed Foss. Or . . .

ELAINE: The nice thing . . .

ROBERT: You robbed him.

ELAINE: . . . is . . . that you will never know. Professional thieves, unlike screenwriters, have no ego, they feel no need to leave their names emblazoned all over their work. *(Short pause)* Tell Jeff when you see him that this is the bare minimum of what—Never mind. *(She writes a note and places it on the table)* Excuse me, I have to finish packing. *(She exits)*

ROBERT: Malcolm? . . . Baby . . . ? Please . . . Oh . . . Oh . . . Malcolm . . . *(Robert's eyes dart among the plants; he yanks up one by the roots, uses his penknife to shave bits of the root into his hand, pops them in his mouth. He chews for a moment, then spits them out, wiping his tongue on the back of his shirt)* No . . . *(He takes a swig of bottled water from Elaine's carryall, then spits it out)* No. *(Again. He stares into the bag. Pause. He looks at Elaine's note)* Malcolm? . . .

(Silence. Robert shaves off more of the root, turns to face the house before removing the salad container and lifting the lid, dropping in the bits. He is replacing the lid when Elaine reemerges with a suitcase. Robert returns the salad to the bag and drops the plant out of sight.)

He wouldn't kill you. It was a joke.

ELAINE: The humor of which—Tell him the story of how you asked me if he would really go through with it, he'll—

ROBERT: He wouldn't.

ELAINE: —enjoy it.

ROBERT: Do you need any help? Packing?

ELAINE: You really do have a problem with anger, don't you?

(She spots one last item she wishes to take; as she retrieves it, Robert lifts the travel bag and brings it to her.)

You know how to lock up?

ROBERT: I should go.

ELAINE: Yes.

ROBERT: I'm sorry.

(Pause.)

ELAINE: Yes.

(Pause.)

Robert's apartment. Robert alone.

ROBERT: I gave it all, everything over to god . . . gave everything up . . . She would or she wouldn't eat it. Either way . . . I gave it . . . then threw up for over an hour, nothing coming up but air . . . offering it . . . The knife I threw off the San Diego Freeway . . . offering it, too . . . My fingerprints were on everything, but then they would be . . . I offered them . . . Her note in its entirety reads: "This is nowhere near what you deserve." Having written enough of them in my mind, I know what a suicide note should sound like. I offered them all, all of them up to god . . . *(Pause)* There was no Malcolm, none I could see. To lose him again . . . Maybe he was there, beside me screaming: NO! Stop!, don't, life, every breath of it is precious, you mustn't kill so much as an *ant* . . . NO! ROBERT! *(Pause)* Maybe.

(Loud knocking.)

But I couldn't hear.

JEFFREY: ROBERT! OPEN UP, I NEED TO TALK TO YOU. ROBERT!

(More pounding. Jeffrey enters.)

What did you do? What did you say to her?

ROBERT: Elaine?

JEFFREY: What did you show her?

ROBERT: Nothing.

JEFFREY: I don't believe you.

ROBERT: I'm sorry about that.

JEFFREY: What did you do? TELL ME!

ROBERT: I just went there over for our meeting and she was all riled up . . .

JEFFREY: Oh, yes, you did nothing, you said nothing.

ROBERT: No.

JEFFREY: Nothing to her at all.

ROBERT: No, I'm sorry, I—

JEFFREY: *YOU* are sorry? Do I seem enshrouded in illusion to you, Robert? I'm—Do I seem less real to you? If I'm making sure my children and wife and I and our grandchildren, all of us, never have to subjugate ourselves to anyone, can live anywhere, and once in a while I get to make a movie I like—I'm sorry I don't live up to your standards, trouble is I'm bisexual; I like both. You want the truth, but—You're lucky to be all one thing. I'm not. I'm not hiding in my marriage, I need my marriage . . . and not just for business reasons, Jesus Christ, half of Hollywood is out of the fucking closet, they're all on the cover of magazines, proclaiming their pride, it's not the old days . . . Were you so . . . ? I'm sorry I've corrupted your poor little . . . Give back the million if it makes you so unhappy you have to . . . piss in other peoples' wells.

(Pause.)

ROBERT: I . . . did not say anything to Elaine. She was very freaked out . . . She was packing . . .

JEFFREY: Yes, I got the note. I'm using your phone.

(Jeffrey dials during:)

ROBERT: She said she figured it out. I said I was very very sorry.

JEFFREY: You have no reason to tell me the truth. *(He hangs up)*

ROBERT: I have no reason to lie. *(Pause)* If she told you I said something—

JEFFREY: She said you faxed her something.

ROBERT: That would be . . . I don't have a fax machine. Remember?

(Pause. Jeffrey dials again.)

JEFFREY: Liz? Any . . . ? What? No, tell me . . . Tell me now . . . No. No. No. No . . . God . . . Oh . . . Liz . . . Noooooo. No. Please . . . Say . . . *Oh! No!* . . . It can't . . . Say this is not . . . true . . .

ROBERT: "We learn from our suffering to reduce and finally eliminate its cause." They died . . . senselessly . . . his children, the woman he loved . . . slammed into a concrete divider at seventy miles an hour . . . dead for no reason . . . Reaching out to stop it, nothing he or anyone could do . . . Maybe now someone understands. No one to take the blame for these terrible deaths . . . Dead for no reason . . . And this time I'm god.

JEFFREY: Help me. All of them.

(Robert comforts him.)

ROBERT: I know . . .

JEFFREY: She drove them into a wall. How could she . . . Oh . . . Oh . . .

ROBERT: "No one owns the life that flows through them . . . anymore than the electric lightbulb owns the electricity that flows through it . . ." *(Pause)* No one.

―――――

Robert alone.

ROBERT: They wouldn't even look for the poison in her blood-stream. Perhaps it wasn't even there. Perhaps she just lost control of the vehicle. Or turned the wheel . . . Perhaps there was a bee in the car . . . Who knows? *(Pause)* We have no control. *(Pause)* The movie of course did not do well. Because I hadn't stuck to my guns, my instincts, and followed my own course . . . But each thing, no matter what it is, is a learning—it's an opportunity: to learn the rules. To perform. And I would do well. I will. There are no limits to what I can accomplish. *(Pause)* "All men contain the potentiality of Enlightenment, and the process therefore consists in becoming what you are." *(Pause)* Done.

END OF PLAY

THE DYING GAUL was written in twelve days in the summer
of 1996. My boyfriend at the time, Patrick William Barnes,
suffered through every minute of it and subsequent assaults
that the play received through a year of constructive criticism. I thank him. I also wish to thank by name the extraordinary array of artists and friends and artist-friends who
helped me steer the play out of its hiding place: Mark
Brokaw, Doug Aibel, Linda Emond, Tim Hopper, Cotter
Smith, Tony Goldwyn, Robert Emmett Lunney, Jerry
Patch, Deborah Eisenberg, Wallace Shawn, André Bishop,
Peter Manning, Michael Wilson, Joe Mantello, Tony
Kushner, Rosalyn Elisabeth Coleman, David Stone, Susan
Gallin, Michael John La Chiusa and Diana Carulli. Lastly, I
extend my thanks to Mark Lamos, Greg Leaming and the
Hartford Stage Company for commissioning the play.

Now some people, albeit a minority, encountered the
play for the first time and liked it *up to the point it turned vio-
lent.* (This may have included the *Times* critic, who seems
like a very nice man who much preferred my play *Prelude to
a Kiss.* I agree, it's a lovely play. I hope we'll see a lot of it in
years to come, and also that its virtues won't prevent me
from writing other, perhaps even *different,* plays as time goes

on.) These people felt the play's resolution was unearned. It was "too surprising." This same resolution implies a harsh judgment of the choices made by the play's central character, a seemingly lovely gay man who had never hurt anyone before, who was in fact a "victim" of terrible loss. Whatever its intrinsic value, this criticism of the play's final destination speaks volumes about those who leveled it. Where did so many of us learn to believe that the victims of terrible loss are ennobled by their suffering? Though I'm sure some people are ennobled—me, I've come out of the experience rather the worse for wear.

My lover, my best friend, my closest colleague over decades, my mother, my father-in-law and another several dozen friends, ex-lovers and colleagues all died rather horrible deaths in rapid succession, and I did not find myself ascending into a compassionate, giving place, but instead a significantly meaner and less generous one. And this play is the best that I could make of my newfound insights into the nature of the beast—the human one. Aristotle thought it was edifying to watch terrible things happen to noble people. Why this should be so, I do not know. But you've got to hand it to him for noticing the phenomenon.

The Greek concept of *Ate* is one that few people seem to remark on anymore, but which is entirely familiar to anyone who has suffered grievously, or celebrated their own boundless desires. Or both. This is a play about *Ate*, at least in so far as I view it. Every single day the TV and newspapers and movies tell us there will be no cost for our myriad purchases.

I don't agree.

—CRAIG LUCAS
April 1999

WHAT I MEANT WAS

AND OTHER ONE-ACTS

WHAT I MEANT WAS

For Connie Weinstock

What I Meant Was premiered on October 23, 1994 at Primary Stages in New York City. It was directed by Seth Gordon. The cast was as follows:

HELEN	June Ballinger
J. FRED	Richmond Hoxie
FRITZIE	Dan Futterman
NANA	Estelle Kemler

■ CHARACTERS ■

HELEN, 49
J. FRED, her husband, 47
FRITZIE, their son, 17
NANA, Helen's mother, 77

. . . but he would have us remember most of all
to be enthusiastic over the night,
not only for the sense of wonder
it alone has to offer, but also

because it needs our love. . .

—W. H. AUDEN
In Memory of Sigmund Freud

Helen, J. Fred, Nana and Fritzie are at the dinner table in their suburban kitchen. All but Fritzie are frozen, reaching for plates, mid-conversation. Fritzie looks front; he wears jeans and a flannel shirt, untucked.

FRITZIE: It's 1968 and we're at the dinner table in Columbia, Maryland—about eighteen miles southwest of downtown Baltimore. Upstairs on my parents' dresser is a photograph inscribed to me from J. Edgar Hoover the year I was born. My mother has gone over the faded ink with a ballpoint pen so you can be sure to still read it. On this wall in another eight years will hang a letter to my mother from Gerald Ford, thanking her for her letter of support. Right now we're in the middle of discussing the length of my hair and the clothes I have taken to wearing. The year before this I painted my entire bedroom black. Here then is everything we meant to say.

(The others unfreeze; they calmly eat their food and affectionately address one another throughout.)

J. FRED: What I think is probably at the root of our discomfort with your favoring long hair and denim is that for your mother and me and also for Nana, because we all survived the Great Depression and in some way feel we triumphed over that—coming from the working class and from immigrant stock, and because so much effort went into that struggle . . .

FRITZIE: Yes.

J. FRED: . . . and we know in a way that you probably never will know what it means to go hungry and to have to work with your hands . . .

FRITZIE: Probably not.

HELEN: Let's hope not.

J. FRED: . . . it seems an affront to our values to see you purposely dressing like a hobo. For that's what denim is, the costume of laborers, the unemployed. When we have seen so many people forced into that position very much against their will.

FRITZIE: I can understand that.

HELEN: And for dad's generation and mine, the idea of protesting a war which our own government has deemed to be necessary, much less desecrating our flag or burning your draft card, again flies in the face of so much we consider essential to our being.

FRITZIE: Yes.

HELEN: I know that a time will come when we will all look back and we'll say, "Perhaps this war was ill-advised," and, "Wasn't that quaint that we were so upset about the way Fritzie dressed," and we will recognize that we were probably as upset about the fact that you were growing up and we were going to have to let you go as we were about your hair which, in the final analysis, is absurdly superficial.

J. FRED: Yes, and your mother and I were also trying to grapple, in admittedly inchoate fashion, with the subterranean knowledge that you were, and are, homosexual.

FRITZIE: I know.

HELEN: And we didn't want you to live a lonely persecuted existence which, after all, is all we were ever told about the lives of gay people.

FRITZIE: And I know, Dad, that I most likely made you feel in some way personally culpable, as if my sexual orientation were some cruel whim of fate, implicitly criticizing you for having been a special agent for the FBI which did so much to help contribute to our national perception of gays as threats to society.

J. FRED: Of course, I can see now with the benefit of hindsight, and the education which you have so patiently provided, that my activities in the bureau, though they may have added further burdens to the lives of many gays already freighted with discriminatory laws and at least one whole millennium worth of religious persecution, didn't actually make you gay.

FRITZIE: No.

NANA: But you know, what I notice in all of this: Fritzie is struggling with the normal tensions and fears any adolescent would be having, regardless of his sexual orientation.

FRITZIE: Thank you, Nana.

NANA: And he is also trying, since he knows he was adopted, and now also knows that he was an abandoned baby— (To Helen) And though you didn't tell him that until you felt he could assimilate the knowledge in a way that wouldn't be destructive to his sense of self-worth.

FRITZIE: And I appreciate that.

NANA: Still Fritzie is searching for an identity, and that can't be a simple matter in a family which in many ways has hidden its own identity, and even fled from its roots.

HELEN (To Nana): Yes, by converting from Judaism to Christianity, you were effectively deracinating all your offspring and their progeny as well.

FRITZIE: But I can understand why Nana wanted to do that. Growing up Jewish in the Deep South at the beginning of this century can't have been easy for her; and then the subsequent scorn heaped upon her by her sisters for what they considered to be her cowardice.

HELEN: And you know Nana's brother was homosexual.

NANA: Well, we didn't call it that; we didn't call it anything back then.

HELEN: When I married your father, Uncle Julian told me he thought your dad was "gorgeous." I was terribly embarrassed, and I wish to this day I could take it back and hug him and tell him that we loved him, no matter how he made love.

NANA: But I think we've made it difficult and confusing for Fritzie at times—and at this very table—by referring to some of my relatives as "kikes."

FRITZIE: I guess it was hard for me to understand where all this animosity towards the Jews was coming from, especially from you, Dad, because you weren't hiding anything; none of your relatives are Jewish, are they?

J. FRED: No, but you know how illiterate and ignorant my mother was. Well, you didn't really.

HELEN: No, I made your father ashamed of her, because I was; she was so uneducated, uncultured. Perhaps dad thought he could distance himself from the Jew he knew I was by—

J. FRED: My mother didn't want me to marry your mom.

NANA: I had called her up and told her we were Jewish. *(To Helen)* Because I didn't want to lose you. I didn't think I should be alone.

FRITZIE *(To J. Fred)*: Mom's having ovarian cancer and the burden of keeping that secret from her and from me when I was eleven must have fueled some of your anger as well. You must have wondered how you were going to manage if she died, and been looking for someplace to vent that rage and fear.

J. FRED: Yes, I think I was.

FRITZIE: I can't even imagine what that was like for you.

HELEN: You know, I think in a sense I must have known it was true. That I *was* sick. Because the doctor wouldn't give me any hormones, and sex was so incredibly painful. I begged him. *(To J. Fred)* I thought if I didn't give you sex, you might leave me.

FRITZIE: Maybe that's another reason why you and daddy drank so much.

HELEN: Well, Nana drank. And my father.

NANA *(To Fritzie)*: Everyone. And you will, too. And take LSD and snort cocaine. And risk your life by having sex with hundreds of strangers in the dark on the broken-down and abandoned piers of New York, even after the AIDS epidemic begins. You watched us losing ourselves over cocktails and cigarettes and thought, "That's what adults do." You wanted to justify our actions, make us *good* somehow, by emulating us.

FRITZIE: I think all that's true. And Mom, I want you to know I understand that the only reason you wanted to sleep with me and would crawl into my bed until the day I left for B.U. and snuggle up against me and kiss me and breathe your liquory breath so close to my face was that you yourself were molested by your dad.

HELEN: I was.

J. FRED: We've all seen and survived terrible things.

FRITZIE: In some ways I feel, because so many of my friends have died now—

J. FRED: Well, your first *lover*.

HELEN: And your second.

NANA: And Tom is sick now, too.

FRITZIE: Well . . . I'm more prepared to face my own death than you'll be, Mom.

J. FRED: Well, we have thirty years before she gets lung cancer.

FRITZIE: But Nana already is senile.

(Nana nods.)

And all of us are alcoholics.

HELEN AND J. FRED: Yes.

HELEN: Well, not Nana.

NANA: I'm not really. I wasn't.

(Fritzie kisses Nana on the cheek.)

FRITZIE: You were the first person I really knew who died.

J. FRED: No. My mother was the first.

FRITZIE: Oh, that's right.

J. FRED: I think you didn't say you were sorry the night we told you she was dead because I never held you or told you I loved you, and you had no idea how to relate to me emotionally.

FRITZIE: I really didn't. I didn't know what I was supposed to say. When I saw you cry at her funeral, I couldn't imagine what was wrong with you. I thought you had a foot cramp. Literally. It was so shocking—that contortion seizing your face in the middle of your walk back from the casket.

J. FRED: I do love you.

FRITZIE: I love you.

J. FRED: And I forgive you for saying it to me so often when you know how uncomfortable it makes me feel.

HELEN *(To J. Fred)*: And I forgive you for never saying it in fifty years of marriage. For saying "Phew!" which, if you recorded it and slowed it down, might sound like "I love you." "Phew!" "I love you!" but to ordinary human ears sounds like "Phew, I didn't have to say I love you!"

J. FRED: And I forgive you for not having children, for being afraid.

HELEN: And I forgive you for not magically knowing the doctors were wrong about my kidneys being too weak, and for not being able to take that fear away, or any of my fears, because you were in some ways more afraid than I.

NANA: I forgive you all for screaming at me when I couldn't remember anything. *(To Helen)* When I picked up the knife and tried to stab you.

HELEN: I understood.

NANA: And for putting me in the home.

FRITZIE: Mom, I'm sorry I threw the plate of pasta at you and called you a "cunt."

HELEN: I'm sorry I said your therapy wasn't working.

FRITZIE *(To J. Fred)*: I'm sorry I embarrassed you by doing the cha-cha in the outfield and being so disinterested in and poor at sports.

HELEN *(To Fritzie)*: I'm sorry we didn't let you know it would be okay if you turned out to be gay.

NANA: And an atheist.

J. FRED: And a Communist.

HELEN: And I'm sorry I told you your father hated homosexuals when it was me, and it was only fear and ignorance.

FRITZIE *(To J. Fred)*: I'm sorry I asked if I could touch your penis the only time we ever took a shower together, when I was four. I know that freaked you out.

J. FRED *(To Helen)*: And I forgive you for getting lung cancer.

FRITZIE: I do, too.

NANA: I'll be dead by then. *(To Fritzie)* I forgive you for calling me a racist pig when I said Martin Luther King was an uppity nigger.

FRITZIE: It's the way you were raised. *(To Helen)* I forgive you for telling me that my career was more important than going to the hospital in Denver with Tom when he had AIDS-related TB and that was the only place he could get treatment, and for suggesting that I should let him go by himself.

HELEN *(To Fritzie)*: I forgive you for lighting the woods on fire. And for making me feel like such a failure as a mother up until and even including this very instant.

J. FRED *(To Fritzie)*: And I forgive you for what you and I both know you did once and I can't say, or you'll probably be sued.

FRITZIE: Thank you.

HELEN *(To Fritzie)*: And I forgive you for trying to kill yourself and leaving that awful, long note saying your father and I were "NOT TO BLAME" over and over. I forgive you for pretending you didn't know me when I walked into the wall of plate glass at your grade school and broke my nose.

FRITZIE: I forgive you for not being the parents I wanted—articulate and literate and calm.

HELEN: People who knew how to use words like "deracinate."

J. FRED: "Inchoate."

NANA: "Emulate."

J. FRED: I forgive you for being ashamed of us, for telling us that you were going to look for your natural parents; I forgive you for never finding them and, being so horrified at whatever you found, you had to come begging our forgiveness.

HELEN: I do, too. And for telling everyone that I pushed you onto the stage and saying to Deborah Norville and Bryant Gumbel that you were gay when I asked you not to. When I said I would lose all my friends if you did.

J. FRED: Well . . . it was important.

FRITZIE: And you didn't. Did you? Is that why you seem so alone now?

J. FRED: No.

FRITZIE: Did I do that?

(Helen looks at him for a moment. She gently shakes her head.)

J. FRED: Love is the hardest thing in the universe. Isn't it?

(Pause.)

NANA: No.

(They stare, lost in contemplation. Fritzie gently kisses each of his parents on the cheek.)

END OF PLAY

UNMEMORABLE

■ *For Maria Aitken* ■
and Patrick McGrath

■ CHARACTERS ■

EARL
LOIS
ENOCH
ROZ
THEO

■ PLACE ■

The action takes place in a bedroom,
a bathroom and
on a street corner.

We all have strength enough
to bear the misfortunes
of others.

—LA ROCHEFOUCALD

A bedroom. Earl and Lois are about to make love for the first time. Maybe they don't really take off their clothes, but rather behave as if they do. Soon they are doing everything they might do in order to please one another and themselves.

EARL: I'm a little nervous.
LOIS: Me, too. That's natural—
EARL *(Slight overlap, like an echo)*: It's natural.

(A little laugh.)

(Sung) Doing a-what comes naturally!

(A little laugh.)

LOIS: What?

(He shakes his head—nothing.)

EARL: Can I help you with . . . ?
LOIS: Oh. Thank you. I can never . . . This shirt is—

EARL *(Overlapping)*: I have, I'm not—sometimes I'm clumsy with—

LOIS: No, you're not.

EARL: —really little things.

LOIS: Oh. Me . . . either? *(Remembers at once)* Me, too!

EARL: Me, too.

LOIS: Me, too. "Me either."

(They both laugh.)

EARL: There.

LOIS: Thank you.

EARL: That's . . . Once I was reading the Sunday *Times*, uh, you know, Sunday *Magazine*, and I asked my wife, my first wife, my only wife, god, breathe—

LOIS: Breathe.

EARL: I said, "Honey what does the French word 'noise' *(Says it to rhyme with 'nicoise' or 'Oz')* mean?" And she took one look and said, "That is the difficult English word *noise!*" *(To rhyme with "boys")*

LOIS: Oh god. Yes.

(At last they kiss. Enoch's voice is heard, then he is slowly revealed in a separate space, alone.)

ENOCH: Some fucks are memorable for their passionate intensity—

LOIS: Ow. No, sorry, it was me, my—

EARL: Cold?

LOIS: I just startled myself.

EARL: Breathe.

(She does. They relax into it, undressing themselves, each other.)

ENOCH: —their unusual duration, long or short, their surprising settings.

LOIS: Is this light too . . . ?

EARL: No, I like it.

ENOCH: Any unexpected element introduced into the sex act can be said to give it that "shock of the new" which is after all the sine qua non for all art, even the art of lovemaking. The makers in this instance, if their sheer ineptitude can be said to even qualify for such a lofty title, implying as it does some form or aspect of intentionality—

(Earl has exposed his genitals to Lois; she smiles, touching him there.)

EARL: Is . . . ?
LOIS: It's beautiful.

(He shakes his head assuredly—hardly.)

ENOCH: —were amateurish at best. Though, granted, some dazzling work of recent vintage has incorporated the elements of the amateur, one must always feel finally one is in the hands of consummate artists.
LOIS: Are my hands . . . ?
EARL: No.

(She blows on them anyway, to warm them up.
In a separate light, Roz is sitting on the toilet. Theo comes into the bathroom with the paper, he is reading, laughing at something that he wants to share with Roz. They remain fully clothed.)

THEO: Can I come in?

(Roz nods.)

ROZ: It's smelly.
THEO: I'll breathe through my mouth, listen to this:

(He reads aloud as Enoch continues composing his review of the lovemaking between Lois and Earl. Maybe Roz lights a match to improve the scent in the bathroom.)

ENOCH AND THEO: "Only a blind goat might have confused what transpired Friday night between Earl Friend and Lois Herkwiser in her modest, East Village walk-up as implying any element of the consummate, much less the more easily achieved consummation associated with such acts."

THEO: He's talking about coming, in the review!

ROZ: I understand.

THEO: Poor Earl.

EARL: That feels really good.

LOIS: It's okay.

EARL: Yes.

LOIS: Mmmm.

ENOCH: The requisite moaning, heavy breathing, and more than occasional gasps—

(A gasp.)

—were laid on with a trowel.

THEO: Listen to this.

(He reads along with Enoch.)

ENOCH AND THEO: "Mr. Friend's 'friend' is not only small by comparison to others on view in more felicitous venues, but it is also tilted slightly to the side, creating an unintentionally comic aspect to his altogether underdeveloped physique. Ms. Herkwiser's more hidden assets must be said to have remained hidden throughout, at least to this viewer. Her nipples are asymmetrically placed, a feature she neither mines for potential comic value nor comments upon, leaving one with the sad suspicion that no one has ever pointed it out to her, and she leads her life in a delusion. If she were perhaps more physically adept, more adventurous in spirit . . . a momentary blowjob so brief as to be missed by any number of spectators who glanced down at their programs is the evening's most 'experimental' touch."

(We see this. Earl is incredibly grateful for it.)

ROZ: Oh, can you imagine?

(Theo is laughing.)

ENOCH: The desultory conclusion of the act—

(Earl ejaculates prematurely, hitting Lois in the cheek and hair.)

LOIS: Oh.
EARL: Oh god, I'm sorry, that—
LOIS: It's okay.
ENOCH: —is not even sordid or surprising enough to report.
EARL: I didn't know I was going to do that.
LOIS: It's okay.
EARL: I didn't go in your—
LOIS: No, no, no, no, no.
EARL: I'm sorry.
LOIS: Please, that's . . . It was . . .
EARL: Here.
LOIS: It was sort of exciting.
EARL: It was?
LOIS: Yes.
EARL: I really like you. Obviously.

(They laugh.)

LOIS: I like you, too.
EARL: Oh god.
ENOCH: This reviewer left before the intermission—
THEO: Oh, Jesus Fucking Christ.

(He throws the paper down; Lois and Earl dim.)

THEO: Poor Earl.

(Theo leaves the bathroom as Roz stands to wipe her butt, several times, checking the toilet paper until there are no stains. She then flushes. Simultaneously:)

ENOCH: —to catch the final act of Roz Wallaby's famous stand-up wipe, which, for all its dexterity and economy has lost some of its original patina. One almost wishes she had not achieved such early notoriety, for it has surely kept her repeating what by now can only be called a tic where others have moved on to explore deeper realms of human idiosyncrasy. Still there is a quaint and familiar comfort in the sound of her flush, and the brio with which she still refuses to wash her hands at the evening's conclusion is a bracing reminder of her capacity for the shockingly original and antiauthoritarian gesture.

(Lights dim on Roz. On a street corner, Theo and Earl come upon one another.)

THEO: Hey.

EARL: Hey, there.

THEO: How ya doing?

EARL: I'm great, how you doing?

THEO: I'm fine. You're sure you're okay?

EARL: Yes.

THEO: Okay.

EARL: Why? Wouldn't I be?

THEO: Well . . .

(He decides better of it—never mind.)

EARL: What?

THEO: I just . . . Oh, I mean, why do we give them the power?

EARL: Who? Is it out? I haven't seen it!

THEO: Oh.

EARL: Oh god, what did he say? Was it—?

THEO: *(The worst, by reputation, entirely silent, unvoiced)*: Oh, yes.

EARL: Did he kill us?

THEO: Well, I mean, no, it's all right, I mean, it's short. I didn't read it that carefully.

EARL: Oh, I've got to get a copy, what did he say about Lois?

THEO: He . . . I don't really remember.

EARL: Oh, it's really bad.

THEO: Well, it's not . . .

EARL: It is.

THEO: *(A shrug)*: Fuck him.

EARL: No, thanks. I got to get to Lois before somebody calls her—

THEO: Listen, I'm sorry, I—

EARL: No, somebody was bound to, say hi to Roz.

THEO: Yes, I will.

(Crossfade. Roz has called Lois to give her the bad news.)

ROZ: I think people will see this, I think this will make people want to go, I do.

LOIS *(In shock)*: Oh my god . . . Is that all? Is . . . ?

ROZ: No, there's . . . *(Pause; throat clear; reads)* "If she were perhaps more physically adept, more adventurous in spirit . . . a momentary blowjob so brief as to be missed—"

LOIS *(Overlapping, near tears, quiet)*: Oh no!

ROZ: Oh, everyone knows he's left his wife for a man and is a total closet case and a frustrated playwright. Come on, don't give him the power, honey, I mean it.

LOIS: Finish it.

ROZ: ". . . By any number of spectators who glanced down at their programs is the evening's most 'experimental' touch." You're sure you want me to—?

LOIS: YES.

ROZ *(Big sigh—this hurts me more than it does you)*: "The desultory conclusion of the act is not even sordid or surprising enough to report." Blah blah—

LOIS: Every word. Please.

ROZ: "This reviewer left before the intermission to catch the final . . ."

(She stops short. Pause.)

LOIS: What? What did he say?
ROZ: I have, I have to call you back.
LOIS: What does he say?
ROZ: I'll call you.

(As Roz hangs up, the two men return to their women, each with a fresh copy of Enoch's review.)

EARL: Baby.
THEO: Darlin'?

(Roz reads to the end, is devastated; perhaps she cries; Theo comforts her.)

EARL: Who was that? Roz?
THEO: You read it?
LOIS: She just couldn't wait.
THEO: Oh.
LOIS: Absolutely glowing with compassion.
EARL: For who?
THEO: Oh, honey.
EARL: You or her?
THEO: I know.

(Lois doesn't understand.)

EARL: She didn't read you . . . ?
THEO: Nobody reads him.
EARL *(Reads)*: "Roz Wallaby's famous stand-up wipe, which . . ."

(From memory, Roz quotes from the review, along with Earl:)

EARL AND ROZ: ". . . for all its dexterity and economy has lost some of its original patina."
THEO *(Overlapping)*: Shhhhhh, shhhh.

(Lois's jaw drops.)

EARL: "One almost wishes she had not achieved such early notoriety, for it has surely kept her repeating what by now can only be called a tic—"

ROZ: A tic!

EARL: "—where others have moved on to explore deeper realms of human idiosyncrasy."

THEO: You can't give him that power.

EARL: "Still there is a quaint and familiar comfort in the sound of her flush, and the brio with which she still refuses to wash her hands at the evening's conclusion . . ."

(Earl and Lois begin howling with laughter, wiping tears away. Roz and Theo are clinging to each other for comfort.)

THEO: People love you.

EARL: Don't you love that?

LOIS: God.

ROZ: God. Poor Lois!

(And suddenly, on a dime, it all flips, and:)

LOIS: My nipples!

(Earl is comforting Lois, and Roz and Theo are laughing.)

ROZ: ". . . The evening's most experimental touch!"

(Roz and Theo are nearly wiping away tears.)

EARL: Oh, baby you have beautiful nipples.
       (Remembers, with glee) ". . . The sound of her flush!"

(And now they are all four laughing, howling, silently. In a separate light, Enoch bows to imaginary applause.)

END OF PLAY

THROWING YOUR VOICE

— To Michael Bronski —

Throwing Your Voice premiered December 6, 1991 at New York City's Naked Angels as part of their Naked Rights festival. Sets were by George Xenox, lighting by Brian Mac-Devitt, sound by Aural Fixation/Guy Sherman and costumes by Rosi Zangales. It was directed by Jace Alexander. The cast was as follows:

RICHARD	Tim Ransom
LUCY	Jenifer Estess
DOUG	David Marshall Grant
SARAH	Lisa Beth Miller

■ CHARACTERS ■

RICHARD

LUCY

DOUG

SARAH

LITTLE SOUTH AFRICAN GIRL'S VOICE

■ TIME AND PLACE ■

After dinner.

After dinner. Lucy, Doug and Richard have coffee; Sarah has
herbal tea. She is hugely pregnant. Gentle music plays on the
sound system; it will end at some point and no one will rise to put
on another CD.

RICHARD: Yeah, but to have them killed? Or maimed?
LUCY *(To Sarah, offering honey)*: Honey?

(Sarah shakes her head.)

RICHARD: To *pay* somebody to do that for you? I mean, I
 understand killing somebody in the heat of passion.
 Or if they had something you had to have.
LUCY: They did.
DOUG: But they did.
RICHARD: Yeah, I guess . . . But, no, I guess I actually have no
 trouble imagining killing somebody when they walk in
 the middle of the subway stairs in front of you really
 slowly—
LUCY: Yes.
RICHARD: —and are just incredibly fat— *(To Sarah)* Not you.
 These people have eaten themselves to this— *(To*

them) And, you know, you try to go this way, they
move—
DOUG: Right.
LUCY: They're doing it on purpose, just to incense you.

(Pause. The music plays.)

DOUG: . . . Or those jerks who block the aisles at Food
Emporium, staring at some foodstuff—
RICHARD: Those are the ones.
DOUG: —as if they'd just woken up from a fifty-year sleep
and are trying to pick the really—right . . .
LUCY: They're having a stroke, probably.
DOUG *(Overlapping slightly)*: . . . brie . . . No, they're not hav-
ing a stroke. Why would you take their side? I hate
those people.

(Lucy smiles.)

LUCY: You're right. They should die.
RICHARD: I just . . . I don't know . . . to *pay* somebody . . . to
kill the mother of your daughter's main competition
for the cheerleaders so she'll be too distraught to audi-
tion . . . It worries me.
DOUG: Well, it's passive-aggressive.
LUCY: It is.
RICHARD *(To Sarah)*: Are we going to be like that in sixteen
years?
SARAH: Mm-hm.
RICHARD: Plotting . . . living our entire lives through little
Grendel? Having no life of our own?
LUCY: She should've killed the daughter's friend directly.
DOUG: That would've—
LUCY: That would've been healthier.
DOUG: Don't you think? Little Grendel? Is that what you call it?
RICHARD: Mm-hm.
LUCY: But . . . you know . . . if I think about it . . . I would
probably . . . if I thought I could get away with it?

DOUG: Uh-huh?

LUCY: I would do the exact same thing to <u>Orrin Hatch</u> and <u>Arlen Specter</u>. WHO ARE THEY?

SARAH: Yes.

LUCY: Wouldn't you?

(Sarah nods.)

Kill their mothers so they're too distraught to go the Senate.

SARAH: Yes. Or . . . actually I've thought about it . . . and I would make them . . . take old rusty fishing knives used for cleaning, you know . . . squid—

LUCY: Mm-hm.

SARAH: —or . . . And I would make them cut each other's tongues out and eat them live on television while Anita Hill stands over them and . . .

LUCY: Screams.

SARAH: No . . . Actually, I would have her, I mean, I think it would be best if she just, you know, *shit* in their bloody mouths. Don't you?

(Tiny beat before:)

RICHARD: Dinner was delicious, thanks . . . Being pregnant has brought out such a warmth of fellow feeling in Sarah.

LUCY: No, come on. They're horrible people.

RICHARD: It's very moving. Yes, they are. Horrible. *(Beat; to Doug and Sarah)* What is this?

LUCY: It's . . . *(She looks at Doug)*

SARAH: It's beautiful.

DOUG: Schubert?

LUCY: Schumann?

RICHARD: One of the Shoe People. No, don't get up.

(Lucy moves toward the sound system.)

LUCY: No, I wanted to get some water. Anybody else?

RICHARD: No, thank you.

SARAH: No. Thanks.

LUCY *(Overlapping)*: Schumann.

RICHARD: Schumann?

DOUG: But . . .

LUCY: Doug?

DOUG: No. Thanks. But . . . if you think about it?

RICHARD: Mm-hm?

DOUG: This whole thing about not wanting to get caught? To *get* the other person but not to be held responsible?

SARAH: Uh-huh?

DOUG: Like the woman in Texas? She wanted what she wanted but she didn't want to—

SARAH: Right.

RICHARD: Exactly.

DOUG: It's like . . . I don't particularly . . .

LUCY *(Returning with water)*: What is this?

DOUG: I was saying . . .

SARAH: The woman in Texas.

DOUG: I don't particularly want, say, to go to Iraq and kill a hundred thousand Iraqis even if I do think their president is . . .

RICHARD: A menace.

DOUG: Well, I don't know what I think, because Iraq is one of the few countries in the Middle East that isn't in the Middle Ages. I mean, women don't have to walk around with bags on their faces and people can vote, can't they?

RICHARD: I don't know.

doug: But . . . anyway, I don't want to see the faces of the people, the children, we kill.

RICHARD: Right.

DOUG: So I pay taxes to a government which pays an entire underclass to go—

RICHARD *(Simultaneously)*: Right.

SARAH *(Simultaneously)*: Yes.

DOUG: —and do it for me, so I can still have my air conditioning in the summer.

LUCY: Which, of course, we don't have.

DOUG: I mean, it's sort of the same. It's still murder.

LUCY: I think that's ridiculous.

DOUG: I know you do.

LUCY *(Overlapping)*: I'm sorry. I think if we hadn't done it he would have eventually blown us all to smithereens or we would have all—history would have been set back centuries by this crazy man and the Iraqi people— *Wait*—are responsible for their actions and their own nation and I'm sorry they're all dead. That's all.

(Pause.)

DOUG: My point . . . was only that . . . we often . . . people often pay other people to do their dirty work so they don't have to look at the consequences—

LUCY: Yes.

DOUG: —of their actions.

LUCY: I don't think it was dirty work. I think . . .

DOUG: It was God's work?

LUCY: We don't agree on this subject.

(Pause.)

RICHARD: But . . . you know? Okay: one way, too, of looking at it is that people . . . if everyone was actually responsible for their own actions and—

DOUG: Well—

RICHARD: —nothing else. If the woman in Texas were *not* held responsible, even though she paid this guy—

DOUG: Legally?

RICHARD: Legally, morally, any way. If . . . See, I didn't go to Iraq.

DOUG: But you paid taxes.

RICHARD: Yes. But—

DOUG: And you *pay* taxes—

LUCY: Let him finish.

DOUG: Wait, you pay taxes to support a government that practices murder in this state. Capital punishment.

LUCY *(Simultaneously)*: There's no capital—

RICHARD *(Simultaneously)*: Not in New York.

DOUG: No?

LUCY: There's no death penalty in New York State.

RICHARD: No.

DOUG *(Overlapping)*: Are you sure? That's right.

LUCY *(Overlapping)*: Not for twenty years.

DOUG: Well, there goes my argument. But . . . I mean— *(To Sarah)* Would you buy fur?

SARAH: With what?

DOUG: If you could? . . .

SARAH: If I could? No.

DOUG: No? Would you buy . . . ?

LUCY: I would. And I would wear it in grandeur.

DOUG: We know you would. But you're poor and you'll always be poor . . . W—?

LUCY *(Singing)*:
Marat we're poor,
And the poor stay poor.

DOUG: That's right.

SARAH *(Overlapping)*: Right!

(Sarah joins her and they sing together:)

LUCY AND SARAH:
Marat don't make us wait anymore!
We want our rights!

DOUG: Thank you.

LUCY *(Singing)*:
And we don't—

(Sarah has momentarily forgotten the words; she rejoins Lucy on:)

LUCY AND SARAH *(Singing)*:
—care how!
We want our revolution
Now!

(Lucy and Sarah crack up.)

DOUG: Yes, me too. All right . . .

LUCY: I can't believe it!

DOUG: Just tell me: would you buy—

LUCY *(Mouthed, silently)*: I still know those words.

SARAH: I know!

DOUG *(Overlapping)*: Would you buy coffee from Colombia if
    you knew— *(To Lucy)* Where is this coffee from?

LUCY: D'Agostino's.

DOUG: If you knew people had died . . . culling it.

LUCY: Harvesting.

SARAH: No, I suppose . . .

RICHARD: But wait.

LUCY: Culling?

RICHARD *(Overlapping)*: Wait, wait.

LUCY: Dougie, you always do this. It was so peaceful here.

DOUG: We're not having a bad time. Are we?

SARAH: No.

RICHARD: No.

LUCY: But you're gonna make all the people feel bad.
    They're gonna go home—

DOUG: No, they're not.

LUCY: —feeling guilty and defiled and sorry they weren't
    born in Ghana.

RICHARD: But. I just . . . Here's my point.

lucy: Okay.

DOUG: Okay.

RICHARD: If people were responsible for their own actions
    alone . . .

DOUG: No one's unhappy.

RICHARD: If the soldiers who went to Iraq—

DOUG: I understand.

RICHARD: —were wholly responsible for their going there
    and I didn't feel any responsibility whatsoever.

DOUG: But you're saying that you do.

RICHARD: Yes, I do. But I'm als—I'm saying that's stupid.
    Even if I agreed that it was entirely wrong for them to
    go there which . . . I don't know about—

DOUG: You don't.

RICHARD: No. But let's say . . . I voted for George Bush and I supported the war . . . totally . . .

DOUG: Okay.

RICHARD: I still . . . in an existential way . . . don't think I should be responsible for someone else's actions.

(Pause.)

DOUG: Would you invest in South Africa?

RICHARD: No. Well, yes, I shouldn't—I already have.

(Beat.)

DOUG: Have—?

RICHARD: That's probably where . . . I mean, I don't know, that's probably where Sarah's ring is from. I didn't ask when I bought it, I was all of twenty-two. *(Pause)* But . . . *(He looks at Sarah)* I've read that most diamonds, new diamonds come from there.

(Pause.)

DOUG: Well, okay.

LUCY: It is okay, don't say it like that.

RICHARD: I also read that . . . people are killed in the diamond mines. Children, for all I know. It's horrible. And I didn't know. What are we supposed to do? *(He looks at Sarah)* I'm sorry. It's probably not. I'm just . . . for the sake of argument—

DOUG *(Overlapping slightly)*: Okay. But would you buy ivory then?

RICHARD: No. But I also wouldn't throw away *old ivory*, if I had it.

DOUG: You wouldn't?

RICHARD: No.

DOUG: Why?

RICHARD: Because I think the damage is already done.

DOUG: But then you're saying there is damage.

RICHARD: No—

DOUG: I caught you! You admit—

RICHARD: No, I'm saying, *if* there's damage, if you're right, which I don't agree with—

DOUG: You do and you don't, you mean.

LUCY: Arlen Specter here.

RICHARD: The damage, you've already paid for the ivory or the diamond or—

DOUG: But if you keep it and treat it as if it's precious, somebody else could sell it someday, thus contributing to the ivory market, thus contributing rather directly to the slaughter of elephants.

RICHARD: Well, I think that's kind of . . . a long chain of command.

DOUG: But it is that. You're still in command. You sell that diamond someday, if it's from South Africa—

RICHARD: Oh, come on, look—

LUCY: Doug.

(Pause.)

DOUG: What?

(Pause.)

RICHARD: I think . . . when you boycott a nation, the entire economy suffers. Including the poor people.

(Silence. The music has ended.)

And I don't think . . . because I buy a diamond . . . I mean, first of all it's the only thing I've ever bought that's worth anything.

DOUG: Fine.

SARAH: Don't get defensive.

RICHARD: I'm not. Have you ever even taken it off, though? In eight years?

(She shakes her head.)

LUCY: Ohhh. That's so romantic.

SARAH: I don't think I could get it off now.

(She tries to test it; Richard stops her.)

RICHARD: Don't. You'll break the spell. *(Pause)* Though you'll probably have to when the baby comes, because we're gonna probably need the money.

LUCY: Ohhhh.

RICHARD: I mean . . . Is that what we should do?

DOUG: No, Richard.

RICHARD: If . . . Here. If I knew for certain . . . for *sure* that someone had actually died in the mining of this diamond. A little thirteen year old black girl . . . a *pregnant* thirteen year old black girl—

LUCY: Oh, please.

RICHARD: —who had to work in the kitchen of one of the mines . . . and she stole a sliver of diamond, this very diamond, to pay for the baby . . . and was beaten for it . . . beaten to death. *(Pause)* Should I get rid of the diamond? *Not* sell it because that would contribute to the diamond mine?

DOUG: I—

RICHARD: Should we just . . . throw it in the gutter?

(Pause.)

DOUG: I wouldn't presume to tell—

RICHARD: Where are your *shoes* from, Doug? Where was this wonderful meal grown? Do you know? Do you check all the labels?

DOUG: No.

(Pause. No one moves.)

LUCY: Look, let's everybody kiss and—

(Sarah's head makes a sudden, sharp turn.)

What? Are you okay?

(Sarah nods.)

RICHARD: That's all. I'm just . . .

DOUG: I understand.

LUCY: So—

RICHARD: I mean— . . . I'm sorry. I guess you hit a nerve. *(To Lucy)* What? Kiss and make up. Yes.

(He makes a kissing noise at Doug.)

DOUG *(Overlapping)*: We're not fighting. You can't stand it if people disagree. Unless it's you.

(Doug makes a kissing noise at Richard.)

RICHARD: My father left me exactly twenty-five thousand dollars in his will and I went out and bought the diamond for Sarah. That was all the money I've ever had at one time and probably ever will.

(Pause.)

SARAH: Does anyone hear that? . . . I'm sorry.

RICHARD: What?

SARAH: Like . . . a *voice?*

RICHARD: A voice?

SARAH: Is someone throwing their voice?

RICHARD: Time to go.

SARAH: Stop! Don't everyone look at me like I'm Joan of Arc. Ever since I gave up caffeine and alcohol, I have this buzzing. *That.*

(They all listen.)

DOUG: I know what it is. *(He stands)* I hear it too.

SARAH: You do?

DOUG: Yes. It's the stereo.

LUCY: That's right.

DOUG: It picks up police signals.

SARAH: Oh, thank god. Uh! *(She sighs with great relief)*

RICHARD: What did you think the voice was saying?

SARAH: It was screaming, actually.

RICHARD: It was?

SARAH: Yes.

RICHARD: My little mystic. *(He takes her hand in his)*

SARAH: God.

RICHARD: That was probably Joan of Arc's problem, she was picking up police signals. Don't you think?

LUCY: It drives me crazy. We hear it at all hours. It doesn't even have to be on.

DOUG: Yes, it does. *(He sits back down)*

RICHARD: Okay?

(Sarah smiles, weakly. Then, her expression changes.)

What . . . ? You still . . . ?

(Sarah looks down at her hand in Richard's hand; she pulls her hand free and sees the ring. She lifts it to her ear. She gasps.)

Oh very funny. Fine, get rid of the ring, I don't care.

SARAH *(Overlapping)*: "Don't hit me!" Listen! *(She holds the ring out to Richard)* Listen to it!

RICHARD: Yeah, I'm sure.

SARAH: I'm sorry, I hear something, I can't help it.

(Lucy takes Sarah's hand and leans in, listening to the ring. At the same time:)

RICHARD: No, it's fine.

(Sarah listens again, then covers the ring with her other hand.)

You all have your little joke.

(Lucy shakes her head: she doesn't hear it.)

It's been a lovely evening. Thanks.

SARAH: You don't . . . ?

(Sarah puts the ring to her ear again. Softly at first, we hear:)

LITTLE SOUTH AFRICAN GIRL'S VOICE: Don't hit me! Please don't hit me!

SARAH: Nobody hears that?

RICHARD: I think we should go.

(The tiny voice screams a bloodcurdling scream.)

LITTLE SOUTH AFRICAN GIRL'S VOICE: Please! Please god! Don't hit me!

(Sarah tears at her finger, removing the ring and throwing it down. The voice screams without words under:)

RICHARD: What are you . . . ?

SARAH: I don't want it! I don't want the ring! Get rid of it.

LITTLE SOUTH AFRICAN GIRL'S VOICE: Please!

SARAH: You can *keep it*!

RICHARD: Okay.

LITTLE SOUTH AFRICAN GIRL'S VOICE: Please don't hit me! Help! Help me, god! Please god.

(The others stare at Sarah, who looks back at them. The tiny voice continues screaming as the lights fade.)

END OF PLAY

GRIEF

For Patrick Barnes

Grief was produced by the Lab Theater Company, Inc., as part of their annual All Day Sucker festival, and they premiered it June 7, 1997 at New York City's Circle in the Square Theater (Downtown). It was directed by Michael Warren Powell. The cast was as follows:

JEAN	Delphi Harrington
ADAM	Patrick Barnes
MARK	Lou Liberatore

■ CHARACTERS ■

JEAN, 60ish
ADAM, 33, Jean's son
MARC, 36, Jean's son

■ PLACE ■

Jean's living room, a pristine room
which has rarely been used.

Even the dead flowers must be groomed and honored,
and by leaving them we leave death,
and those are the attachments of this world.
Fear be gone!

—HARRY KONDOLEON
Diary of a Lost Boy

Marc and Adam seated in dark suits.

JEAN'S VOICE *(From off)*: I need to do something with my hands, please, Marge, go home now, I'll be all right, I promise, goodnight now, thank you for everything, I mean it, bye bye.

(Door closes. Jean enters in dark clothes. She sits. Long pause. Adam cries quietly. Marc reaches out to comfort him.)

ADAM: You were so great.

MARC: What do you mean, I didn't do anything.

ADAM: Mom. You were. You really were so incredible with everyone. I was so, well, I wasn't amazed, I mean, I wasn't surprised, you're always great, but you handled everyone with such respect and care and you kept giving to them as if it was all their loss and not yours too.

(Short pause.)

MARC: He's right. You were so nice to that guy from the nursery who kept blubbering and what was the deal with him, you'd think dad was his brother or something.

ADAM: We spent a lot of money there. *(Pause)* All those fruit trees and hedges and annuals every year, and he's the guy who trimmed the dead limbs off after that big storm and who sprayed the birches for birch miner every year.

(Short pause.)

MARC: True.

ADAM: But you were really kind to him. And to the people from dad's office, they were all so shook up, and you, I don't know, it felt like you were the strongest person here. I was so . . .

MARC: Me, too.

ADAM: You were great. *(Pause)* You want something to drink?

(Jean nods.)

Coffee?

JEAN: Brandy.

ADAM: You want brandy?

MARC: I'll get it. You want?

ADAM: I'll take a sip.

JEAN: Bring the bottle.

ADAM: Mom.

MARC: Okay.

ADAM: She's teasing.

MARC *(Exiting)*: Whatever.

ADAM: Just a sip. *(Pause)* You doing okay? . . .

(She nods.)

You're amazing. *(Pause)* You are. *(Pause)* He's seeing all this.

(Jean rises, moves to the CD cabinet, puts on her church gloves and starts taking out CD cases. At the same time:)

You don't have to wear gloves with CD's. Here, I'll do it, what do you want to hear?

(She takes CD's out of their cases and snaps them in two.)

Don't. You'll cut yourself.
JEAN *(Overlapping)*: That.
ADAM: Mom, be careful.
JEAN: That's what I want to hear.

(Adam watches Jean snap several more CD's in half.)

ADAM: Not all the Mozart, I'll take them. Please.

(Jean picks up a sharp object and scratches the surface of a CD.)

ADAM: What are you doing?

(Marc enters with a bottle of brandy and little paper cups.)

MARC: Music?
ADAM: We have better glasses than that.
MARC: Less to wash up. Whatcha doing?
ADAM: She's, uh . . . Mom, what are you doing?

(She continues, undeterred.)

MARC: Had enough Mozart? Here.

(She takes the glass of brandy and knocks it back in one swig, resumes her destruction of Mozart CD's.)

ADAM: Hey.
MARC *(Silently, to Adam)*: Let her be. Shhh.

(Jean fills her glass a second time.)

ADAM: Mom. Mom!

(Adam stops her from pouring the brandy and takes the glass away from her.)

Whoa, I know it's been a rough day, probably the worst of your life.

(She drinks directly from the bottle—not just a sip, but one long incredible chug.)

Okay, all right, Mom, hold it, hey, that's, you're gonna get blotto.

JEAN: That is not what I'm gonna get.

ADAM: Okay.

(She begins plucking off her jewelry and her uncomfortable clothes.)

MARC: Here's to dad.

(Jean spits on the rug; the boys stop for a moment.)

ADAM: Come sit. Come on, I'll help you with that.

(He urges her into a chair; she continues to strip.)

No, we don't want to see you in your bra.

MARC: Speak for yourself, I wouldn't mind. Joke. It's been a very stressful time.

ADAM: This is post-traumatic syndrome, this is grief. It's okay.

JEAN: I'm three-quarters through my life and what I do is not subject to your vote or his.

(Short pause.)

ADAM: Okay.

MARC: Good for you. Strip down and dance, Ma, we won't judge.

(Pause.)

JEAN: Well . . . You won't be here.

(Short pause.)

MARC: Okay.

(Pause. She removes her stockings.)

ADAM: I'm gonna make a pot of coffee. *(He exits)*
JEAN: Do me a favor.
MARC: Yeah?
JEAN: When he comes back, tell him you back me up on everything.
MARC: Okay.
JEAN: You promise?
MARC: Promise.
JEAN: It's important.
MARC: Okay.
JEAN: Oh my god, if I never hear that word.
MARC: What word?
JEAN: "Okay." We use it, in this house we use that word to mean everything but "okay." We use it to convey displeasure, confusion, irony, rage, we use it to mean "not okay, but hey, I don't want to stir the water, now is not the time," but now is the time, I'm going to stir up all the water and all the snakes are going to swim free, so watch your ankles.
MARC: Oka—

(He stops himself before the whole word can get out. She laughs; Adam returns.)

ADAM: What's so funny?

JEAN: You.

(Short pause.)

ADAM: Okay.

MARC: Mom says we overuse it, the word.

ADAM: What? "Okay"?

JEAN: That's the other interesting thing to me. I actually didn't say anything about overusing the word, I say we use it to lie sort of about what it is we are indeed saying, for instance now when you came in and I was laughing, you asked, "What's so funny?" and I said "You," and you didn't like that but you said "Okay."

(Pause.)

ADAM: All right.

(Pause.)

JEAN: Your father never wanted children. I convinced him that it was a good idea, no, no, that's not true either, I said I'd leave him, and we had children, and of course we know the end of that story.

ADAM: What does that mean?

JEAN: I'm talking. "Okay." He thought you were both completely disappointing, but he was scapegoating each of you in his way because he was disappointed, he was disappointed in himself, but it was not his way to say Oh, I am so disappointed, he took the more interesting tack of making me the villain and you the two little byproducts of my villainy, and I said to myself once if I said it a hundred million times—a galaxy of silent promises from me to me—that if he died before me I would bury his memory, not, oh not just dance on his grave, but erase him, and every ounce of what he stood for is dead with his paltry, wiggly awful flesh, all of it dirt and mud in the ground, and wherever his spirit is, the other spirits are running fast and furious to escape him, because your father is the black hole of bad karma and he is dead! *(On the last word, she pours brandy all over the sofa)*

ADAM: Mom.

MARC: That's silk.

JEAN: Oh, it's ruined, we'll have to throw it out.

(She jabs at the silk with her nail file, puncturing it over and over. Pause.)

ADAM: Whatever you don't want, I'll take.

JEAN: No. No one will have anything. I will destroy whatever I wish to destroy because your father has left everything to me; I convinced him that you would both bleed me to death if I got sick or distracted or weak, and so he has left everything in my name, and it is entirely up to me what I will leave to you and what I won't leave to you, and first things first: the furniture, the paintings, the whole hideous lot of Chinese scrolls, ivory carvings and bonsai along with all the signed letters from Schubert and Napoleon and Ulysses S. Grant will go the way of the Great Auk.

ADAM: Are you . . .

JEAN: And Marc backs me up, he supports me.

(Short pause. A nod from Marc.)

You can try to have me declared insane, but for this purpose I have been seeing a psychoanalyst for the past two years, from the instant your father's X-ray first spelled out the words "Oh Joy, Oh Rapture," in fact, I have seen two psychoanalysts and joined a support group as you know and told them all you might both try to undermine me in this, so they have agreed, each of them, to testify on my behalf, and your father also went on record with our lawyers about insisting I be the sole executor, and that neither of you was to be allowed one word on the subject of his estate, finis. It is entirely up to me. Everything. Of this I am exultant, and of what I am about to tell you. Your father was a freak of nature. He liked nothing more than to give me a long, slow enema; he was a pig, and I put up with it forever and forever, don't ask me what I was thinking, it had something to do with the way people talked on *Jack Paar* and, no, *Mike Douglas*, and something to do with thinking there was going to be some sort of parade which has not taken place—on my behalf. There have been other parades to celebrate war, killings, and we marched in those. You are both out on your own, you are so extraordinarily old to be living here with me, your sexual and spiritual shenanigans are no longer any of my business, we're burning everything, every last penny of all this horse shit which has constituted my . . . life.

(Pause.)

MARC: What are you so angry about?

ADAM: Thank you.

JEAN: "Thank you." When anyone in this house speaks any form of brutality which represents the venal interests of another shareholder, somebody, that somebody who didn't think of the mean thing to say *first* says "Thank you," as if some brilliant stroke—

ADAM: Stop talking like this, where are you getting all this?

JEAN: All of "this," Adam, comes out of my imagination and my heart which you have never glimpsed, this may in fact be the only glimpse you ever get of me, so you might want to shut up.

ADAM: They've put you on something.

JEAN: Oh, well, I can see that you are interested in doing all the talking, and we know where you learned that. I will give you both until Friday morning to pack up your things, if you touch one object of mine or your father's,

I will have you arrested, I have already informed the police that there may be trouble.

MARC: The—what?

ADAM: Police.

MARC: I heard her.

ADAM: She's spoofing.

JEAN: In the eighth grade there was a girl named Cheryl Chepenick and when her boyfriend dumped her she mailed him his windbreaker all cut up in little pieces, and each little piece was wrapped around one of her turds, so she got a reputation for being kind of scary, and I thought she was nuts, but in fact, she went on to win an Olympic gold medal and she's married to a brilliant violinist in Berkeley, California, and she's perfectly happy, she's in this issue of *People*, and I was the one who never sent anyone any turds, until now, but I'm saving mine, and you're going to get them, all of them, at once, in a big shipment from America's foremost movers. You think I'm joking. Let me just also say that I loved you both dearly when you were little, when you had puppets and Slinkys, but when I saw that you were going to use them against me the way that you did—

ADAM: Use them against you?

JEAN: You will of course not remember that I bent down to kiss you when you were this big, so perfect, and I held you, and you hit me so hard in the eye with your Slinky I had to have stitches.

ADAM: No.

MARC: You did.

JEAN: I didn't want you to feel bad, we kept it from you. Protecting you. And *you* will not remember that you called me a stinking gash the first time you got drunk and I found you here with that woman from Radnor, in my bed. I honestly don't know where you got that at sixteen, but I know where you got the inner conviction that I would ultimately have no recourse, that your father would never believe me, not over you; you got that from me and all from me, because I never believed I could do anything, I never thought I was entitled, not even to breathe, I was raised to believe that I was born to serve, I am the last of the Mohicans who said nothing when you each began to date pale, moronic versions of my pale, moronic self. And now we're all of us all all all alone.

(Pause.)

ADAM: Mom. This is good you're getting all this off your chest.

MARC: Dad did stuff to us, too. And you just stood by. *(Short pause)* He beat the shit out of us. And more. *(Pause)* And you knew, too. Didn't you?

JEAN: I knew . . .

MARC: You did.

JEAN: . . . that I was the brunt of every imaginable put-down, and I would laugh and laugh, because I can't do anything, I don't know how to type or use a computer or an answering machine or program a VCR, because I am the "dumbo." Isn't that what you called Gail when you divorced her, you did, and you always said Teal was stupid, you said it to her face. Oh, that is so funny that mommy can't spell. Ha ha ha ha, if you or your brother had to suffer through some form of emotional or physical humiliation at the hands of that cretinous heir to his father's stockpile of completely unearned stock dividends then I can only say there are support groups for everything.

(Pause. Marc starts to cry. Jean sings and sways, clapping her hands:)

We are the world!
We are the children!
Here in Pennsylvania,
People are mean.

Everybody knows it!
But they're all churchgoing!
I hope they fry!
I'll light the flame!

ADAM: You're . . . this is . . . you're not yourself.
JEAN: No?
ADAM: This is funny!
JEAN: I think so.
ADAM: I'm . . . delighted.
JEAN: No, you're not, you don't want to have to move out.
    But you do. Have to. Friday. By five.

(Pause.)

ADAM: Can I say something? . . . I knew what he did to you.
    Kids know everything. I found the enema bag. I heard
    you crying, lots and lots. How would I know I could
    come to you? Was there ever any indication that we
    could talk to you about anything? We all learned the
    same rules from the same master.
JEAN: Yes, but the difference is that your rules were different.
    Yours favored you, hence you still think you can live
    here and contribute nothing and that you're actually
    entitled to something.
ADAM: And what is it you think?
MARC: Don't do this, guys.
ADAM: What is it you think?
JEAN: I think . . . that someone is going to have to pay. And
    that it is, this time it is not. Going. To be. Me.
ADAM: Okay. I'm sorry. Not okay. Why does it have to be
    Marc and me?

(Pause.)

JEAN: Because, honey, you're boys. You're my boys, and
    you're not bad people. Well, I mean, yes you are, you
    are really quite an atrocious person. I think Americans

by and large have become the world's, I mean, you're not alone, let's say that. I do not feel that I am significantly different than you are. And I admire a winner, which is why I am going to do everything, *everything* I can to win out over you. You're just close enough and I know all your weak places and Marc's and you don't deserve it, and I'm going to do it. I'm going to watch you. From a distance. Marc's going to back me up in this, too.

(Short pause.)

ADAM: Did you guys have some sort of a preliminary . . . ?

JEAN *(Overlapping)*: If . . . after a bit of time . . .

ADAM: Did you?

JEAN: I feel that you are someone I want to be associated with, I want to stand up in public anywhere and say, That's my son, instead of making the kind of excuses I made for you forever, and you, Oh, Marc was sick, Marc had his paper route, he won't do it again, it was the other driver's fault, that girl was sleeping with other boys as well, Adam didn't mean to torture the white mouse to death, Adam can't find work, there's a depression, oh dear, his wife left him for another woman, that teacher had it out for them both, because they're rich and happy and beautiful, but actually now, see, neither is beautiful, they look like what they are, alcoholics and and potato chip fiends, even golf is too much for the two of you, so you will have to prove to me that you are beautiful on the inside, which is something I gravely doubt—

MARC: STOP THIS!

JEAN: That was authentic. Marc. Meaningless, but . . . Get worthwhile jobs, do constructive, loving things; I'm going to burn all the vestiges of your father, I'm going to sell the house, and move into an apartment, and give the money to charity, every cent, and if you want my love, you can earn it. And I . . . will try . . . to earn

my own. For the first time. At the grand old age of . . .
(She says her age, but runs her hand over her mouth, garbling the words) I will try . . . to deserve my own respect.

(She exits. Pause.)

MARC: Remember that queer kid, Antony, who used to give all of us blowjobs after dark under the bleachers?

(Pause.)

ADAM: Yeah?

(Pause.)

MARC: I always think about him.

(Pause.)

ADAM: What?
MARC: I think that's what mom's saying.

(Pause.)

ADAM: Did you both take something?
MARC: He was just . . . you know . . . looking for something diverting and . . . tender. And . . . in a sea of, um, not very happy people with, you know, money and the threat of seventy years of . . . primetime TV . . . he wanted something warm to put in his mouth.

(Pause.)

ADAM: But . . . Marc, you broke his nose.

(Pause.)

MARC: I know. *(Pause)* But god . . . I wish he was here.

(Pause. Jean returns with a trash bag. She begins taking framed letters off the wall and knickknacks off shelves and drops them in the bag along with her jewelry.)

ADAM *(To Jean)*: That letter is worth thousands.

(Jean puts a silver candlestick through the letter, pulls the letter out of its frame and rips it to shreds before depositing it in the bag along with the candlesticks.)

ADAM: Goodnight.

(He leaves. Marc looks out at us.)

MARC: Mom did everything she said she was going to do. We hired expensive lawyers on contingency, naturally, and we lost; several expert witnesses convinced the judge that she was not incompetent, and then she did in fact give all the money—nine million dollars—to charities . . . and she moved into a retirement community . . .

(Adam reenters with a trash bag and helps his mother. He takes off his watch and school ring, takes off his tie, his belt with the silver buckle, his diamond earring, and drops them all into the trash bag.)

. . . and Adam . . . I haven't heard from Adam. He helped with the bonfire. Then . . . pshyoooo. *(Pause)* I stay in touch with mom . . . I clean up for her and, you know, do stuff in the little garden they've allotted her . . . we watch videos . . . I cook . . . And I found the guy—Antony—who used to give the blowjobs. He works for Disney, and makes a lot of money, and he thanked me for the broken nose. Apparently guys told him it made him look like the young Marlon Brando. But he doesn't want to see me.

(Marc drops his own valuables into the bag. Adam looks out at us.)

ADAM: I thought it was just her grief, overwhelming her. And maybe it was. I think she gave it to me, first and foremost, she wanted me to have it. And I guard it. I guard it for her. It's here. All of it. Whenever she wants it back. *(Pause. He touches his chest)* Safe and sound.

(Pause. Jean looks out at us.)

JEAN: Well, it was all actually sort of on impulse . . . When you step into your body for the first time, there is a kind of "Oh." I realized that I was in fact alive. And it was all I could do for the rest of my life to contain my surprise and try not to destroy anyone else. Ultimately I learned I could. And that I regretted nothing. It may have taken me sixty some years, and it isn't always pleasant, experiencing . . . yourself, but it is . . . It's . . . Well . . . *(Short pause)* It just . . . *(Short pause)* Is.

END OF PLAY

THE BOOM BOX

The play is dedicated to Ricky Ian Gordon

The Boom Box, produced by the Lab Theater Company, Inc., premiered November 24, 1996 at New York City's West Bank Café. It was directed by Michael Warren Powell. The cast was as follows:

RICK   Patrick Barnes
JAY   Peter Jacobson

■ CHARACTERS ■

RICK, a ghost
JAY, a ghost

■ TIME AND PLACE ■

The play takes place on the spirit level.
Nothing is visible or audible to the audience
except the two actors onstage.

Jay and Rick, side by side.

JAY: Hey. *(Short pause)* New here?

(A little nod.)

A little overwhelming, huhn?

(Another nod.)

I'm Jay.
RICK: Rick.
JAY: Nice to meet you, Rick.

(Rick looks down at the ground before him, behind him.)

RICK: Wow.
JAY: Oh, you haven't seen it.
RICK: No.
JAY: It's beautiful.
RICK: God.
JAY: Astonishing, isn't it? What they can do?

RICK: Oh my god.

JAY: All the detail . . .

RICK: It's actually . . . incredibly beautiful.

(Rick looks further, at the ground beneath Jay, then all around.)

JAY: All the effort. Well, I mean, take a stroll around the whole place, you won't believe it . . . Before it gets more crowded. *(Short pause)* You didn't see them working on your panel at all?

(A little headshake from Rick.)

Wanted to be surprised? *(Short pause)* What were you . . . I mean . . . where were you when they were working on it?

(Pause.)

RICK: Oh, I was . . . I was taking the Grand Tour.

JAY: Of?

RICK: All the places I'd traveled with my boyfriend . . . Um, some in Italy, some in, oh, you know, all kinds of places . . . Gardens . . . San Francisco . . .

JAY: How long has it been? Since you . . . *[died]*?

RICK: About uh . . . about . . .

JAY: I know, time . . . really—

RICK: I can't get a hold of it.

JAY: Me either. *(Silence. He indicates the ground under Rick)* Are you happy with it?

RICK: That . . . I mean, the whole idea of being satisfied has, it's all changed for me.

JAY: Uh-huh.

RICK: It isn't, what *is* sort of . . .

JAY: *Is.*

RICK: So, yes, I am. Because it's what it is.

(Pause.)

JAY: But not because it's what you would have wanted.

RICK: What . . . I would have wanted has become . . . It's not even as solid as smoke. I can see it in my memory, but it has no substance, anymore than I can touch you or feel this . . . fabric.

JAY: It goes on for miles, literally, square miles now.

(Pause.)

RICK: Let it cover the planet.

JAY: Oh, don't say that.

RICK: Why? We're all coming here anyway.

JAY: Were you surprised?

RICK: What?

JAY: That there was anything. *After.*

(Pause.)

RICK: Surprised, see, that's it, I can remember my wondering, my doubts, and . . . but now . . . It's all . . . It's a movie. Their lives, their movements, suffering, cracked ribs, wars, chapped lips, everything they go through, their orgasms . . . it's a movie. A really long, really complicated, insufferable foreign film. A million times more complicated than one of those Russian epics based on a nineteenth-century novel where everybody has a diminutive and patronymic . . .

(Jay looks at him quizzically.)

Oh, you know, those names like Maria Marinovich, little Maria, what the nurse calls her, her contemptuous sisters . . .

JAY: What kind of work do you do?

RICK: Well, I haven't resumed. I haven't quite gotten the knack of what it is, I mean, why it is we do it here. You see the doctors running around pretending they're taking care of the little tiny dead babies and the teach-

ers teaching the dead babies once they've been pre-
tend-reborn and pretended to grow . . .

JAY: It's just practice.

RICK: It's no more sensible or clear or—I feel less enlight-
ened than I did when I was living.

JAY: This is living.

RICK: Okay.

JAY *(Simultaneously)*: This is just . . . another—

RICK *(Simultaneously)*: A different plane.

JAY: Level. Yeah.

(Pause.)

RICK: I miss fucking.

JAY: Oh, here they come.

(They look off into the distance.)

RICK: I don't look, I never look.

JAY: At the . . . ?

RICK: People.

(Pause.)

JAY: Really?

RICK: Never. I look at buildings. The only living things I can
stand are trees.

JAY: Why?

RICK: They live longer. They don't scream when they're dying.

(Pause.)

JAY: You won't be reborn with that attitude. *(Pause)* Is that
your strategy? *(Pause)* You're making it harder on
yourself hanging around here at your panel if you
don't want to see your loved ones.

RICK: I'm testing myself. Building my resolve. If I can stand
here and see past them, then I can withstand anything.

JAY: But . . . I mean, there's gotta be something better than this . . . limbo here: don't you want to be a saint or break the cycle of rebirth forever?

(Pause.)

RICK: I want the living to come screaming after me and put me back in my life which I loved more than anything anyone has ever loved . . . I want my eyes and my gift for languages and my dick . . . I don't want some antelope's dreams or some politician's glandular problems, I definitely definitely definitely don't want to see what happens in a hundred years because I know what it is already, it's horrible suffering, I want Rick. I want me. I want exactly what I had.

JAY: Well, here . . . I mean, isn't that what they're bringing, don't you want to look—

RICK: At what there is of everything I had except me in the middle of it.

JAY: You didn't love your life. *(Silence)* These are the people who made your life real, and they're right here.

RICK: I was real without other people.

JAY: Then you still are real.

(Pause.)

RICK: I hate the New Age. I was an exception, I was an aberrant burp in a hideous time . . .

JAY: Then wait until Doomsday, you're right . . . Something will come along that deserves you.

RICK: Why do you think they've plunked me down next to you?

JAY: To punish me for accepting too much, this is the ultimate test: how much compassion and wisdom can you extend, here's a real stumper, go, Jay!

RICK: What did you do?

JAY: I was a stock analyst.

RICK: I wrote astrology charts.

JAY: Did you believe in it?

RICK: Oh, I believed in it the way one believes in whatever pays the bills, it was fun when I was an amateur, and then . . .

JAY: Rick . . . ?

RICK: Statler.

JAY: Oh my god! Your column was great.

RICK: Thanks.

JAY: It was so funny.

RICK: Thanks.

JAY: I read it every week, me and my lover.

(Pause.)

RICK: Thanks.

JAY: You were really famous.

RICK: Maybe you'll get your picture in the society pages now. Standing next to the ghost of Rick Statler is the once-devastatingly-handsome-but-now-rather-hazy figure of Jay . . . ?

JAY: Gilson.

RICK: Gilson. Jewish?

(Jay nods.)

JAY: You?

(Headshake.)

What did you—I mean, what were your beliefs?

RICK: I believed in the stars.

(Pause.)

JAY: Oh, listen, somebody's brought their boom box.

RICK: I love this song.

JAY: Me, too.

(Rick listens, then starts to sing along:)

RICK:

Don't talk about love
Don't talk about a wedding ring

(Jay joins him:)

BOTH MEN:

We're here
Right here
Right now
And we only need one thing . . .

I gotta have you tonight
I want to—

(Jay keeps singing, but Rick breaks off, seeing something.)

JAY:

—Do it all
And scale every— . . .

(Jay sees Rick staring.)

What?

(He, too, looks at the unseen figures approaching.)

You know one of those . . . ? *(Pause)* Is that . . . ? You
know him?
RICK: Goddamit!
JAY: What?
RICK: You tricked me.
JAY: What?
RICK: You got me distracted.
JAY: I didn't.

RICK: I didn't want to see him.

JAY: God, he's . . . what a soul.

(Rick wails.)

He can hear you, I swear he can . . .

RICK: He's so beautiful. Look at his nose, I could swallow it whole.

JAY: He does have a nice face, but I mean . . . Look at those thoughts.

RICK: He's playing that fucking song . . .

JAY: Is—? I mean, is that some special song or something?

RICK: That fucking asshole.

JAY: Oh, it's . . . He wants you to know he doesn't regret anything, from the night you met till the morning you died.

RICK: Stop reading his mind, it's none of your business.

JAY: It's all of our business.

(Pause.)

RICK: We should never ever ever have made love, I gave it to him, I GAVE IT TO HIM!

JAY: And he still doesn't regret it, that's the amazing thing.

RICK: I did it, I killed him.

JAY: Just love him and get over yourself. He's still alive. *(Pause)* He's rewinding it. He's going to play it again.

RICK: You should have been a simultaneous translator.

(Pause. Jay starts moving his head to an unheard rhythm, then starts to sing.)

JAY:

I saw you there
You saw me here
Do we need to know more
I need you with me
Your hand in mine
And your clothes on my floor

RICK *(Overlapping)*: SHUT UP, THIS ISN'T ABOUT YOU!

(Silence. Rick watches his invisible boyfriend and listens to the song. Jay is looking around. He sees a loved one:)

JAY: There you are.

(He reaches up and touches an unseen face. Rick is lost in the vision of his lover; he hums along with the song, then sings:)

RICK:

> . . . —Tonight
> I want to do it all
> And scale every height
> I gotta have you tonight
> Who cares about tomorrow
> I gotta have you tonight
>
> Slide up next to me—

(Jay, touching the body in front of him everywhere, kissing it, joins Rick:)

BOTH MEN:

> Rub up against me
> Feel my heat feel my need
> I need your skin
> I need your mouth
> The beast in me must be freed
>
> I gotta have you tonight
> I want to do it all—

(Rick stops singing abruptly.)

JAY:

> —And scale ever—

RICK *(Overlapping, to his lover)*: Take me back! Bring me back! I'd do it again, I'd die again if you'd kiss me again, please.

JAY: He hears you.

RICK: Please, baby . . . Come on, do it . . . I want to be there.

JAY: You are.

RICK: I want to be there.

JAY: You are.

(Rick is punching his unseen lover.)

RICK: You fucking fucking bastard . . . I love you . . .

JAY: He hears.

RICK: I love you so.

END OF PLAY

BAD DREAM

To Sarah Schulman

The first performance of *Bad Dream* was produced by the Atlantic Theater Company as part of their From Love to Sex and Back Again series. It was produced by Hillary Hinckle and broadcast on WBAI radio, May 11, 1992. It was directed by Scott Ziegler and Gordon Hunt. The cast was as follows:

FRANK   Steven Goldstein
MICHAEL   Ray Anthony Thomas

■ CHARACTERS ■

FRANK
MICHAEL

■ TIME AND PLACE ■

In bed. Early 1990s.

Darkness. Emergency horns blaring: a ship in trouble on the sea; water rushing through vents, shouts. Fade to sound of someone breathing. The breaths comes faster, then a quick expulsion of air and a relaxing of breath: the end of a nightmare.

FRANK: Are you awake? *(Pause)* Honey? . . .

MICHAEL *(From a deep sleep, inaudible)*: What'swrong?

FRANK: I'm having heebie-jeebies.

MICHAEL: Ohhhh . . . it's okay. *(Pause)* Tell me . . . *(Pause)* It's gonna be great, you'll see.

FRANK: It won't.

MICHAEL: You have a bad dream?

FRANK: It was horrible.

MICHAEL: What?

FRANK: No, go to sleep.

MICHAEL: It's okay . . . What happened?

FRANK: It was all . . . There was like this . . . It was like this horrible engine room . . . It was filling up with water . . . Every time I tried to turn one of these gears or open one of these portals, they were all too small and there was all this, like, grease . . . It was getting hotter and hotter . . . And you had left me these messages which I had written on my stomach or on my chest—how to get out—and I forgot they were there and I wiped my hands, trying to get this goop off and . . . smeared your words.

MICHAEL: Awww. *(Pause)* Do you . . . ? What do you think the ship represents?

FRANK: I don't know.

MICHAEL: What are your associations?

FRANK: I don't know . . . Just tell me.

MICHAEL: Well . . . It's something large and important . . . You're trapped inside . . . and it's sinking . . . What—?

FRANK: The two-party system?

MICHAEL: De doctor thinks dat maybe what you want is for me to write your report for you . . . save your ship from sinking . . .

FRANK: Uh-huh.

MICHAEL: And that you feel bad maybe because you've been jerking off . . .

FRANK: Where do you get that?

MICHAEL: Well, Freud feels strongly that in a dream . . . sticky goopy stuff . . .

FRANK: I see.

MICHAEL: —almost always represents sticky goopy stuff. And in light of the fact that we have not been having maybe the amount of necessary activity which . . .

(Good-sized silence.)

FRANK: I left the tape in the VCR. Right?

MICHAEL: . . . Yeah, you did, but—

FRANK: I'm sorry.

MICHAEL: It's okay, I don't care.

FRANK: I'm just out of my mind. Nothing makes me feel like . . .

MICHAEL: I don't care, really, it's your body. You can . . . beat it till it . . . blisters . . . *(Pause)* It's a horrible dream. You'll finish your report.

FRANK: Oh, I've put it off so long . . . I mean, I don't have a *clue* . . . Do you want to go to sleep?

MICHAEL: Mm-hm.

(Pause.)

FRANK: I don't even know where *not* to start with it.

(Pause.)

MICHAEL: Is there anything I can help with?
FRANK: Shoot me . . .

(Pause.)

MICHAEL: When is it due?
FRANK: Two weeks ago yesterday.
MICHAEL: You got an extension, I thought.
FRANK: It doesn't matter, because I'll never finish it.
MICHAEL: Yes you will.
FRANK: I'm a complete fraud. I don't know anything about—
MICHAEL: You always say this—
FRANK *(Continuous)*: —this kind of system. I've been bull-shitting my way through—
MICHAEL: You always do this and then you forget you do it.
FRANK: Not like this.
MICHAEL: Yes, you do. And you always say that.
FRANK: I do?
MICHAEL: Yes. Remember we went to Maine and you were in a panic about that thing—
FRANK: I wasn't like this, though.
MICHAEL: You were out of your mind. You wished Catherine a belated happy birthday and apologized—
FRANK: Right.
MICHAEL *(Continuous)*: —for forgetting and it was like three days after the party you threw.
FRANK: Yeah. *(Pause)* I was.
MICHAEL: You were certifiable. Remember you rented that horrible shack up at that lake because—
FRANK: Uh!

MICHAEL: —you *had* to be away to learn that software and then you called your answering machine . . . ?

FRANK: No.

MICHAEL: Oh, there was a message from the phone man saying they'd buzzed the buzzer and you were sure the dog had destroyed the apartment—

FRANK: Oh, yeah.

MICHAEL: That drove him nuts and you called the super and had him check on the apartment and the dog was with *you?*

(Pause.)

FRANK: Thank you. I feel better.

MICHAEL: Good.

(Pause.)

FRANK: I am. I'm insane.

MICHAEL: Sweet dreams.

(Pause.)

FRANK: They're going to fire me, though, I know they are. I'm sorry.

(Pause.)

MICHAEL: They just gave you a raise.

FRANK: That's why. They're paying me too much and the recession . . . *(Pause)* I just . . . My mind, one thing to the next: I won't finish the report, they'll fire me, I won't be able to keep up our bills, we'll lose our health insurance . . . *(Pause)* When you do you have your blood done again? *(Pause)* Sweetheart? *(Pause)* You can't be asleep yet.

MICHAEL: I'd like to be.

FRANK: Just tell me.

(Pause.)

MICHAEL: Last week, Frank.

(Pause.)

FRANK: When were you gonna tell me that?
MICHAEL: When you were back on the planet.
FRANK: Is it bad?
MICHAEL: It's not great.
FRANK: You can tell me.
MICHAEL: Fifty-six.

(Pause.)

FRANK: Oh, baby . . .
MICHAEL: It's okay. Ken says a lot people walk around for years with low T cells. I just . . . have to keep doing the pentamidine—
FRANK: Right.
MICHAEL: —and . . . resting and eating right and . . .
FRANK: That's right. Oh sweet baby . . .
MICHAEL: I feel fine . . . The ship isn't sinking yet.
FRANK: I know.
MICHAEL: You'll survive . . .
FRANK: I know I will.
MICHAEL: I know you'll miss me. *(Pause)* You'll meet somebody great.
FRANK: I don't want to meet somebody great.

(Pause.)

MICHAEL: Your report'll be great.
FRANK: You're great.
MICHAEL: Yes, I am. *(Pause)* So are you.

(Silence.)

FRANK: I love you.

MICHAEL: Shut up. *(Pause)* Please?

(Frank is crying, trying not to make any noise.)

Come on.

FRANK: I'm sorry. I'm sorry.

(Michael turns on the light.)

MICHAEL: Why do you do all the crying and I'm the one who's sick?

FRANK: I know.

MICHAEL: Please stop, honey.

FRANK: I can't.

MICHAEL: All right.

FRANK: I can't even imagine a world without you.

MICHAEL: I can't imagine a world without me either.

FRANK: You must be so fucking angry with me.

MICHAEL: I'm not, though.

FRANK: I know you're not, that's the amazing thing.

MICHAEL: I'm glad you're not sick.

FRANK: But why? *(Pause)* Why aren't I sick? It doesn't make any sense. I've slept with half of America.

(Pause.)

MICHAEL: You know something?

frank: What?

MICHAEL: I'm sick of feelings.

FRANK: Me too.

MICHAEL: I'm sick of support groups.

FRANK: Me too.

MICHAEL: I'm sick of sickness. I'm sick of articles. I'm sick of the news. I'm sick of constantly being reminded. I'm sick of Magic Johnson.

FRANK: Oh, he's so cute, though.

MICHAEL: And funerals. I'm sick of me.

FRANK: I'm not.
MICHAEL: I am.
FRANK: I'm not.

(They kiss.)

MICHAEL: Can we . . . ?

(Frank nods, wiggles eyebrows.)

I meant turn out the light.
FRANK: Oh.
MICHAEL: Sorry.

(Frank turns out the light. Pause.)

But we can.
FRANK: Really? . . . You sure you want to?
MICHAEL: Well . . .

(Rustle of sheets.)

FRANK: God, I have never known anybody who could get
hard so fast.
MICHAEL: Yeah . . .
FRANK: Ooof.
MICHAEL: Play with my balls . . . *(Pause)* Mm.
FRANK: Can I suck you?
MICHAEL: No.
FRANK: Please?
MICHAEL: No, Frank.
FRANK: How's that?
MICHAEL: That's great. *(Pause)* Let me lick you . . . Bring it
up here . . .
FRANK: Wait . . . Be careful, your beard . . .
MICHAEL: Did I scratch you?
FRANK: No, just . . . Oh, that feels so—*God.* Yes, suck me . . .
Wait . . .

MICHAEL: Come.

FRANK: No, with you.

MICHAEL: Come on my face.

FRANK: Are you close?

MICHAEL: Uh-huh.

FRANK: Are you sure? Are you ready? . . . Oh, Jesus your mouth feels so . . . Ouch . . .

MICHAEL: Did I—?

FRANK: No, it's okay . . .

MICHAEL: Are you sure? Do you want to look at it?

FRANK: No. I want this, I want to make you come . . . *(Breathing, rustling)* Oh, I love you.

MICHAEL: I love you too . . .

FRANK: I love you so much.

MICHAEL: Oh yeah . . . Oh . . . Oh . . . Oh . . .

FRANK: Shoot it . . .

MICHAEL: Yeah . . .

FRANK: Yeah . . .

MICHAEL: Oh . . .

(The sounds of Michael's orgasm. Overlapping the end of it:)

FRANK: Baby . . .

MICHAEL: Jesus . . .

FRANK: Did you . . . ? *(Cracks up)* Did you shoot in my *hair*?

MICHAEL: Did I?

FRANK: Are you like working for NASA or something?

MICHAEL *(Also laughing)*: Did I really? It didn't get in your eye or anything.

FRANK: I don't think you can get it from your eye, can you?

(Frank turns the light on. With the blanket up over his knees, Michael wipes himself up; the tissues are treated like nuclear waste.)

MICHAEL: Don't you want to come?

(Frank takes the tissues from Michael and deposits them in the trash bin.)

Wash your hands.

(Frank goes off. Sounds of water running. Michael lies still. Frank returns.)

FRANK: Can you?
MICHAEL: What?
FRANK: Get it from your eye.
MICHAEL: No. Did you get it in your eye?
FRANK: I don't . . . I can't tell . . .
MICHAEL: Did you rinse it?
FRANK: Yes. I'm fine.

(They kiss, snuggle, lights still on.)

Goodnight, honey.
MICHAEL: Don't you want to come?
FRANK: Maybe in the morning. *(Pause)* Lights out?
MICHAEL: I might read.
FRANK: You sure?
MICHAEL: Mm-hm.

(Frank has his head on Michael's chest.)

FRANK: You're the best.
MICHAEL: Yep.

(Pause.)

FRANK: This feels so good. *(Pause)* I don't give a shit about the report.
MICHAEL: Good.
FRANK: It'll write itself.
MICHAEL: Right.

(Michael sighs. Frank's eyes are closed. Silence.)

Honey?

FRANK: Mmm?
MICHAEL: Never mind.

> *(Silence. No one moves. Lights fade.)*

END OF PLAY

IF COLUMBUS
DOES NOT FIGURE IN
YOUR TRAVEL PLANS

— To John McDermott —

A bar, empty but for Geoff, who is preparing to close up for the night. News playing on the TV creates a flicker of light from above. A stranger in a rain slicker enters.

GEOFF: Closed, sorry. Just missed last call. The register's cleared.

(The stranger pulls his hood down, revealing a handsome face. We hear Geoff's thoughts, as we will throughout, alternating with his spoken lines:)

(Voice-over) Ooo, cute. *(Spoken to the stranger)* How 'bout a beer on me?

(The stranger gives a little nod; Geoff moves behind the bar.)

That hit the spot? All I got's tap, so . . .

(Geoff checks the stranger's face: the stranger is looking up at the TV screen.)

Oh, yeah. You following this? Two hundred people. *(Makes a quiet crash sound)* They played the pilot's broadcast to the tower? You hear that? Screams his head off. Then they beep out the last word. Like we don't know what it was, right? *(Slides beer toward the stranger)* There you go.

(The stranger drinks the beer without acknowledging Geoff. Again we hear Geoff's thoughts:)

(V.O.) You're welcome. *(Tiny beat. Spoken)* Can you imagine bothering to say "Shit!" when you're about to hit the ground at three million miles an hour in a ten-thousand-ton . . . casket?

(The stranger stares back at him. Beat.)

(V.O.) Strong silent type or serial killer? *(Resumes cleaning up, putting away glasses, emptying the garbage, etc. Spoken)* I don't know, I always think it'd be . . . you know, so great to go gracefully. Right? You think about that?

(No reaction.)

I mean, I've had friends die, dozens, who hasn't these days, right? But . . . *(Almost no pause. V.O.)* Now he thinks you have AIDS. *(Without skipping a beat, again spoken)* . . . Some really surprised me: difficult, whiny kinda guys suddenly turning into Buddha: a peace and acceptance and *generosity*—worried about you, and, like, oblivious to their own pain. I'm sure I'll be screaming bloody murder whenever my plane goes down. Which hopefully won't be— *(Pause)* I mean, I don't know, somehow I managed to be one of the lucky ones who stayed negative all through the whole epidemic, who knows *how*, I mean, not that I'm a slut, well, I'm not exactly a monk either— *(V.O.)* Oh shut up, he's not *that* cute. Oh yes he is. *(Spoken)* So, but I mean, you *know* that shit's gonna happen the minute you get on the plane, right? *(Does voice of stewardess)* "If Columbus does not figure in your travel plans, now would be an excellent time to come forward." If Columbus does not *"figure"* in your travel plans, how the hell'd you get on the plane?

(He waits a beat for the stranger's smile or laugh: nothing. Geoff barks out a little laugh himself.)

(V.O.) He thinks you're psycho. *(Spoken)* So what do you do? . . . Probably an airline pilot. Right?

(The stranger hands him a business card.)

(Reads) Communications Services.

(No reaction.)

(V.O.) Those lips, those eyes. *(Looks at the card again, turns it over)* No name, no . . . address. *(Returning the card, spoken)* I started out in business school, but didn't really have the head for it, I guess . . . The concentration. So I did what every other guy I knew did, you know, more or less: went to the gym, took a coupla acting lessons, tending bar for a while to tide me over, suddenly a couple of years' worth of tips disappear up my nose, decide to clean up my act. Here I am finally: starting to like myself, a little less desperate, you know. One hopes. I don't know. *(Pause)* I'm doing all the work here, chief, is English not your first language or something?

(The stranger smiles. Geoff waits a beat.)

(V.O.) He's yanking my chain.

(The stranger shakes his head slightly side to side; Geoff decides he's imagined this.)

(Spoken) Want to sit here quiet and I leave you alone?

(The stranger shakes his head "No.")

Wanna tell me your name?

(Again the stranger shakes his head.)

(V.O.) Wanna kiss my ass?

(Again the stranger shakes his head "No.")

(Spoken) What was that? You just . . .

(The stranger stares back at him.)

You got a tic or something, you . . . *(Waves it all away: "Never mind")* Wouldn't it be wild if you could really read everybody's mind? If everybody could?

(The stranger smiles slightly, nods.)

(V.O.) Then I wouldn't have to make a fool of myself— tell you how much I want you to take me with you. I'd just *think* it: "Can I go home with you?"

(The stranger nods.)

(Spoken) See, now, I can't tell if you—did you nod right there?

(The stranger nods again.)

You did. At, say, something I . . . *(V.O.)* . . . *thought?*

(Another nod from the stranger.)

(Spoken) Why'd you do that? Just then.

(No response.)

(V.O.) Okay. I'm thinking of a number—the number is *two. (Short pause. Spoken)* What am I thinking?

(The stranger holds up two fingers. Beat.)

Uh-huh.

(Silence as they stare at each other.)

You're not gonna tell me how you do that, are you?

(The stranger shakes his head "No." Pause.)

(V.O.) Thirteen. *(Short pause. V.O.)* Go ahead.

(Short pause. The stranger raises all ten fingers, followed by three.)

(Spoken, a little laugh) Lucky thirteen. *(Short pause)* Cool. Have you . . . been on Leno and shit?

(The stranger shakes his head.)

Course not. *(Pause)* Soooooooo . . . *(He laughs again, nervously)* You really are . . . Okay . . . I'm thinking of a proverb. *(V.O.)* "Love thy neighbor as thyself." *(Short pause. Spoken)* Tell me what it is.

(Headshake.)

You won't?

(Headshake.)

You won't speak.

(A nod.)

Gotcha. *(Short pause. V.O.)* Should I be scared?

(Headshake.)

(V.O.) Should I be . . . amused?

(Headshake. Beat.)

(Spoken) Okay, drink up, we're officially breaking the law here, so . . .

(Geoff crosses to the front door; he holds it open for the stranger.)

Time to say nightie night. Out you go. Come on. Up.

(The stranger does not move.)

Closing time at the OK Corral. Before I have to call the cops.

(Still the stranger does not move.)

We're closed.

(Geoff watches the stranger watch him.)

(V.O.) You waiting to rob me?

(The stranger shakes his head "No.")

(V.O.) No? You wanna . . . what? Do it here?

(The stranger shakes his head "No.")

(V.O.) You want me to leave with you.

(The stranger nods.)

(V.O.) You're gonna take me with you?

(The stranger nods.)

(V.O.) Your place?

(The stranger nods.)

(V.O.) How about mine?

(The stranger shakes his head "No.")

(V.O.) You gonna hurt me?

(The stranger shakes his head "No.")

(V.O.) You sure?

(The stranger nods.)

(Spoken) Be just my luck, right? Always a sucker for a pretty face. *(No pause. V.O.)* I can run out into the street anytime, you know that.

(The stranger shakes his head "No.")

(Spoken) No? I can't?

(Again: "No." Geoff tries to step outside the door. His feet won't move. He strains with all his might.)

I don't know what the fuck—

(Geoff's feet literally pull out of his shoes. As he moves to bolt out the door, the metal gate comes crashing down in front of him, trapping him. Or any other magical effect that defies logic, physics. The stranger sips his beer.)

I thought you said you were gonna take me with you, how are we gonna get out? Please stop. What do you want? You want my body?

(The stranger nods.)

You can have it. You want, what, my . . .

(The unspoken word hangs there for a moment before the stranger nods.)

(Shakes his head) Uhn-un. Get out. Go. Please.

(The stranger downs the last of his beer.)

I'm not ready. What did I do, did I do something wrong?

(The stranger rises.)

I'm being punished! No! No! No! Please? *Please.* Oh please!

(The stranger shakes his head "No.")

It isn't fair, I'm young, I'm healthy, it's too soon! I took care of everybody—everyone died, I took care of all of them. Everybody. I deserve another chance. No! I want a boyfriend. A life. It's not fair.

(The stranger agrees; he shakes his head side to side.)

No. It's never fair.

(*Another side-to-side headshake of agreement.*)

I don't want to go . . . (*Pulls himself together*) Okay. Grace, right? Peace. Acceptance.

(*The stranger nods.*)

You're gonna hold me?

(*The stranger nods.*)

I know you are. And soothe me.

(*The stranger nods.*)

Carry me the whole way?

(*The stranger holds out his hand toward Geoff.*)

Love me?

(*A nod.*)

Okay . . . I'm trusting you on this one . . . (*He begins to move toward the stranger, containing his panic, trying desperately to be a good boy*) God. I'm going out in style. Right?

(*The stranger nods.*)

All yours, big boy.

(*He wraps his arms around the stranger who returns the embrace.*)

Oh shit.

(He holds the stranger's head against his.)

Thank you. Oh god. I've been so alone. Oh.

END OF PLAY

BOYFRIEND RIFF

To Marisa Zalabak

■ CHARACTERS ■

MAN

Lights up.

MAN:

> I loved this guy
> Who worked for the phone company.
> He told me what he did there,
> But I can't remember.
> I think he worked out at my gym.
> I think that's where we met.
> I loved his flattened nose—
> Like those guys in those old obscene drawings
> With the crew cuts and rolled-up sleeves
> And thick lips and tattoos.
> Every one of 'em has the same dumb
> Fuck-me eyes.
> This guy didn't have a tattoo,
> But he had a mild,
> Sweet version of all the rest.
>
> I'll tell you who had a tattoo, though—
> A really beautiful orange
> And blue one of a bird—

Was my friend Geoff
Who I know I met at the gym.
I think we had sex twice.
He was a dream.
What a handsome easygoing guy,
All of maybe five-foot-six.
He worked as a bellhop
In one of the new hotels
While he studied to be an actor.
Then I heard he was in a movie.
And I saw it.
He was pretty good, too.
He once asked me if I would fuck him.
He was nervous about it, he said,
Because he'd never done it.
He didn't say it like it was a line either.
But maybe it was.
I wrote a part for him in a movie
And even called the character Geoff,
But the real one was sick by then
And couldn't do it.
No, that's not right.
He'd already died the week
Before we called
To offer him the part.
It wound up getting cut
From the movie anyway.
The guy who did play it is dead, too.
His mom just sent me a Christmas card
With the news.
He had lesions on his face
When we shot his scenes,
But he'd cover them up with makeup.
I wonder about my friend Geoff, though.
I loved fucking him,
But I wonder if that's what got him going,
Looking for other guys to fuck him

Without a rubber.
This was before we knew,
Wasn't it?
Or when we knew and
Didn't want to know—
That little sliver of time
Between hearing and knowing.
No, I think it was before.
Right before.

But the guy from the phone company.
God, I loved making love to him.
We didn't fuck.
I don't think he was into it.
That's probably why I still used to see him
Around in the mid-eighties—
Maybe once or twice, that's all.
He wouldn't acknowledge me.
Do I look so old?
Did I stop returning his calls?
Did I want to pretend
I never stood naked
On the roof of the pier
With my dick in and out of two mouths,
Liking that people were looking,
Admiring it with its smooth head
Like a shiny purple stone?
But I loved the telephone man's cock.
It wasn't real big
But it was straightforward
And kind of blunt
Like his nose
And his forehead.
I think of him as a Neanderthal
With nice manners—
The kind of daddy your well-behaved friends had
When you were in kindergarten.

Imagine if all the nice daddies died.
Surely they were innocent
And they didn't spread it . . . I mean . . .
Willingly.
That would be inexcusable,
Wouldn't it?
If they gave it to their kids
When they kissed them,
When they were so overcome with adoration
And pride,
Having to clutch each one to their breasts
And plant a loving,
Deadly kiss
To their warm,
Flushed faces.

I just loved that guy from the phone company.

My boyfriend Peter died when I was making *my*
   movie,
We'd separated, and I'd written a part for him,
But we couldn't give him the part,
It was big and we had a tiny budget
And no time for him to get sick
Or hold us up
So we gave him a little part,
But he couldn't play that one either;

I flew out to California to see him in the hospital,
And I was so mad at him for being sick,
For dying,
I made him feel terrible,
I told him it was his fault,
Sort of.

He'd saved my life.
Literally.
I'd tried to kill myself

With an enormous overdose
And he'd found me,
He'd come over and found me
And got me to the hospital just in time,
Even though he really just wanted to break up with me
He'd done that.
And I couldn't save him
Of course.
So I blamed him
And made him feel like shit.

When he was dying he said,
Who's that guy standing in the corner
Over there?
In the hospital room.
I said, Honey, there's nobody over there.
And he said, Phew, that saves me the embarrassment
Of not knowing his name.

But that guy from the phone company.
Very hot.
Taciturn.
I can remember every single thing we did.

But . . . not his name.

END OF PLAY

CREDO

For Robin Bartlett

Credo premiered at Marathon '95 at New York City's Ensemble Studio Theatre. It was directed by Kirsten Sanderson and performed by Marcia Jean Kurtz.

■ CHARACTERS ■

PERSON, male or female

■ TIME AND PLACE ■

Christmas Eve or shortly thereafter,
New York City, the 1990s.

Lights up. Person alone onstage.

PERSON:

So it's Christmas Eve,
I go out with the dog.
Jim and I have just broken up.
I've just been to an AA meeting
Where a woman got up
And said she had no friends,
Her best friend is her VCR
And it's broken.
I came home to the hole where the sofa was.
There's no Christmas tree either.
I can't stand the thought of sweeping up all the dead
    needles
And dragging the carcass out to the street
To join all the other dead trees
With what's happening to the rain forest.
I know the two aren't connected,
But anyway, I pull up a folding chair
And heat up a piece of cold pizza.
This, I think, is the low point.

The walls show little ghosts where the pictures once were.
I go out.

Did I tell you I didn't get my Christmas bonus?
Well, I wasn't expecting it,
But I haven't been able to take Apple to the vet
About her problem,
So she dribbles a little across the lobby,
Past the doorman who isn't smiling at me;
I'm sure it's because I haven't given him *his* Christmas
    bonus,
But maybe it's the trail of urine, too,
I don't stop to ask.
I smile bravely
And step outside where it has of course started to rain.
And people are running and looking very upset.
Surely the rain isn't that bad.
I turn:
There's been an accident on my corner.
I snap my head away,
I know if I look there'll be a baby carriage there
In the middle of the street.
I refuse to look.
They certainly don't need another person standing
    around, not doing anything.
I put my mind . . . Where can I put my mind?
Vienna.
Where Jim has gone with the woman he left me for.
You can't escape these thoughts.
All I know is her name.
Her name . . . is Carmella.
Apparently.
And I believe that she has had a sex change.
As far as I know, this has no basis in fact,
But I believe it as firmly as I believe
That there is nothing wrong with New York City
That can't be solved at least in part by keeping
Cardinal John J. O'Connor out of city politics

And back doing what he really does best
Which, if we are to take his word for it, is:
Exorcisms.

Where,
Where can I put my thoughts?
Ecuador.
My parents are in Ecuador.
They asked me to join them,
And I said
No, Jim and I would be spending the holiday together.
I hope that he and Carmella are caught
In the crossfire of some terrorist . . .
No, I don't.
Not really. But you know:
The sort of thing you see
On the evening news.
If you have a TV.
Or a phone.
Jim stopped paying the bills months ago,
As a kind of secret warning of what was to come.
But I refuse,
In my bones I refuse
To see myself as a victim.
I have gotten myself into this.
I allowed him to talk me into maintaining a joint bank
    account.
Everytime a little voice in my head would say
Watch out.
He's cute,
But he's not that nice.
Beneath it all,
Behind the charm,
His chin,
That first night,
And then again in Barbados,
Beneath it all
Is *him*.

I alone took each and every step
Which brought me here
To this street corner
In the rain
On Christmas Eve
With my dog whose urinary infection
I cannot afford to fix.

And at that moment, my friends,
My dog squats,
And the worst thing that has ever happened to me
Unfolds before my very eyes.
A wire, a loose plug from somebody's Christmas dec-
    orations
Carelessly strung in front of their little tea shop . . .
Electrocutes my dog.
And she falls immediately dead
On the sidewalk
In a sputter of sparks . . .
And the lights go out all down the front
Of the tea shop.
And a man comes out:
"What did you do?"
And I drop to my knees, unafraid,
Let me die, too,
Electrocute me.
And I embrace my dog, Apple,
Whom I have had for sixteen years.
She is my oldest friend.
She has seen me in my darkest, most drunken days.
She has been to every corner of my life, watched me
    make love.
She growled at the dogs on the dog food commercials.
She has been across the country and back.
Apple, I'm not afraid to say, is the purest,
Most uncomplicated expression of love I have ever known.
And she has been killed by an electric current
In the last sick days of her valiant existence.

The man stares at me from above.
"Oh my god," he says.
He can't believe it
Any more than I can believe it.
"Come in," he says.
We carry Apple into the shop.
To me she smells good,
But to some people she does not.
It's been too cold to bathe her.
It's hard for one person to hold her in the shower.
She doesn't like the water.

The man offers me the only thing he has.
Tea.
We talk,
And he assures me that the accident on the corner
Did *not* involve a child.
And no one was killed.

What to do now with Apple?
I can't cry anymore.
I have cried so much the last two weeks
I can't cry for her now.
And I know . . .
In some way I see all at once that
Jim was not really good enough for me,
That I will meet someone else.
And even if I don't I will have
An extraordinary and rich and complicated life.
It is entirely up to me.
I will most likely survive all the roadblocks
and the detours.
As my dad always says:
"Life can be rough, but think about the alternative."

But then again
He's never been sick a day in his life.
He hasn't ever had to struggle just to stand

Or been unable to stop himself from peeing
Where he knows he shouldn't
And doesn't want to,
But there it is in a stream,
Surprising him and me.
He's never had to look up
With big sorrowful eyes which say:
"I had no idea.
Don't yell."

No.
I only hope that I will go as quickly as Apple
When the time comes.
And if I don't,
I will absolutely,
I *know* I will face that bravely
And with dignity.
I know.
And if,
For some unforeseen but totally justified reason,
I can't,
And I am making a complete ass of myself,
Saying things I wouldn't ever say
And acting childishly
And turning into a prude
And a conservative
And am being a complete drag on everyone
For months and years,
I know my friends will forgive me.

And if for some equally valid and twisted,
But ultimately logical reason,
They don't,
Or they can't,
Or they're all dead by then,
Or it's August and they're away,
Then I will forgive them,
Right?

The same way I forgave myself
For yelling at Apple the first time she peed
Before I realized what was going on.

And if . . .
Again, if I can't,
And everything is entirely for shit
And I can't even find my way to the end of a sentence . . .
And . . . you can fill in all the blanks . . .

That will be fine, too.

END OF PLAY

GOD'S HEART

For Dr. Tim, dazzling spirit

God's Heart premiered at Trinity Repertory Company in Providence, Rhode Island, on May 5, 1995. It was directed by Norman René. Sets were designed by Eugene Lee, lighting design was by Debra J. Kletter, sound was by David E. Smith and video was designed by Tom Sgouros, Jr. The cast was as follows:

CARLIN	Ray Ford
JANET/CAROL	Phyllis Kay
DAVID/REESE/CUSTOMER	Ed Shea
ANGELA/WHITNEY	Brienin Bryant
AÑA/VOLUNTEER/NIGHT NURSE	Avaan Patel
ELEANOR	Harriet Harris
BARBARA	Janice Duclos
CASHMERE/DR. FARKAS/VALERIE	Rosalyn Coleman
PATTY	Barbara Orson

God's Heart opened on April 6, 1997 at the Mitzi E. Newhouse Theater at Lincoln Center Theater in New York City, under the direction of André Bishop and Bernard Gersten. Sets were by Robert Brill, costumes by Toni-Leslie James, lighting by Brian MacDevitt, original music and sound by Dan Moses Schreier and David Van Tieghem, and video and projections by Batwin + Robin Productions. The play was directed by Joe Mantello. The cast was as follows:

CARLIN	Ndehru Roberts
JANET	Amy Brenneman
DAVID/REESE	John Benjamin Hickey
ANGELA/LAB WORKER	Kia Joy Goodwin
AÑA/NEWSCASTER'S VOICE/	
NIGHT NURSE/LAB WORKER	Lisa Leguillou
ELEANOR	Viola Davis
BARBARA	Julie Kavner
CASHMERE/DR. FARKAS/	
INTERACTIVE VIDEO VOICE/	
MAN IN PURPLE HOOD	Kevin Carroll
ENSEMBLE	Kisha Howard,
	Brenda Denmark,
	Kim Yancey Moore,
	Akili Prince,
	Peter Rini,
	Pamela Stewart

CARLIN, 15
JANET, 30
DAVID, 30
ANGELA, 16
AÑA, 21
ELEANOR, 30s
BARBARA, 30s or 40s
CASHMERE, 16

(Carlin, Angela, Eleanor and Cashmere are black;
Janet, David and Barbara are white;
Aña is Guatemalan.)

A number of roles are doubled:

PASSERSBY, played by the ensemble
INTERACTIVE VIDEO VOICE, played by Cashmere
NEWSCASTER'S VOICE, played by Aña
DR. FARKAS, played by Cashmere
MAN IN PURPLE HOOD, played by Cashmere
NIGHT NURSE, played by Aña
LAB WORKERS, played by Angela and Aña
REESE, played by David

■ TIME AND PLACE ■

God's Heart takes place after dark in New York City,
mid-1990s.

People are frightened by the thought of getting too much information, which just shows we're not in the Information Age yet. Are you frightened by the thought of getting too much money? Too much happiness?

—ARNO PENZIAS
New York Times Magazine

After a decade in which both the drug trade and police sweeps expanded with similar zeal, forty-two percent of the black men in the District of Columbia, aged eighteen through thirty-five, were enmeshed in the criminal justice system on any given day last year, according to a study made public today.

—JASON DEPARLE
New York Times, front page, April 18, 1992

Carlin seated by a payphone, reading a schoolbook, knapsack beside him. A number of people proceed past on their way to somewhere else. Pause. Carlin looks out at us.

CARLIN: You sit here long enough . . . and people come by: they be like, "Oh, that must be a tree or some piece of furniture I'm walking by." Walking by what, right? Kinda like what they think: all these galaxies out there they can't see? They know how much they all weigh, what gasses and compounds and shit: don't none of it show up on no telescope . . . I can totally identify with that. I know I'm here, right?, whether nobody seeing me or not, that's they problem; get a better set of instruments and take a *look* . . . I'm glad I'm see-through, want to know the truth, you know what I'm saying? . . . Like them night glasses: "I see you, you don't see me!" Yeah. *(Pause)* Sometimes, okay?, I'll be like . . . looking up at all the windows up there—the apartments and shit—and somebody'll come stand in one . . .

(A separate light begins to glow on Janet; she stands at her bedroom window, bottlefeeding her baby and looking out.)

You can only see their shape. Probably one of them same people walking by, never seeing you sitting right in front of their face. I try to imagine what they're seeing now: put myself up there, looking out from the starship, that's their apartment—Hey, you gotta do something to fill up the time . . . And I'll be like checking out the park down below, what's happening in that world: the green, cement land, right? *Earth.* Then, you know, I make up like whole stories in my head about "what if." Like all them science fiction shows, other worlds and all, I love them shits, I do.

JANET: Honey? . . . Have you seen this kid? Sits in our park?

(David appears near Janet.)

DAVID: There you are.
JANET: Have you seen this kid?
DAVID *(Smiles at the baby)*: I've seen this kid . . . Which?
JANET: Down there? See? By the phone.
DAVID: The crack dealer?
JANET: Is he? No, he's so sweet-looking, he *reads.* Don't say he's a crack dealer, please.

(Carlin, looking up, waves.)

DAVID: There you see?

(Janet has returned his wave.)

DAVID: Don't wave back!
JANET: Why?
DAVID: I don't know, just don't, that's all.
JANET: Yes, Daddy.

(David moves back toward the bed, and Janet surreptitiously waves again to Carlin.)

DAVID: Oh, man.

JANET *(To the baby as she moves to join David on the bed)*: You all done? . . . Marguerite?, at work?,

DAVID: Uh-huh?

JANET: . . . thinks you let babies pick up whatever they want, play with it however they like, touch anything: that they have an innate sense of what they can and cannot swallow.

DAVID: Oh, really?

JANET: No, there are books on this. That if you let them follow their natural curiosity and don't startle them, that it's the parents who cause accidents.

DAVID: Uh-huh.

JANET: By teaching them to be afraid. But how do you not do that? How do you keep your fear to yourself?

DAVID: Prozac?

JANET: I don't mean neurotic fear, the ordinary things like falling out of windows which she says a baby won't do, they recognize heights . . .

DAVID *(Laughs)*: Oh my god . . .

JANET: . . . but, no, she says it's true, anyway, but I mean, truly frightening things.

DAVID: Like this theory?

JANET: Okay.

DAVID: No, go on.

JANET: No, I just . . . I don't want Nicky to wind up in some park.

DAVID: Then don't put him out on the windowsill.

(Janet hands David the baby and moves back to the window.)

JANET: And sometimes it seems like nobody's watching the store, that's all. I mean, where are his mom and dad, that kid?

DAVID: Mm-hm.

JANET: He shouldn't be sitting out there at night, whether he's selling drugs or not. Why isn't anyone . . . doing anything?

DAVID: Hey. Hey, come to bed.

JANET: I don't know, you're a doctor, you get to help people in your work, I don't.

DAVID: What do you mean?, advertising helps.

JANET: Right.

DAVID: How else would anyone know what to buy? It's a public service, I'm serious. No, I know what you're saying. You're right. We're incredibly lucky. We are.

(Janet, David and the baby snuggle together on the bed. Below, Angela appears near Carlin. During the scene, David will leave the bedroom.)

ANGELA: Yo, baby G, what's up?

CARLIN: Angie, what's going on?

ANGELA: What you been doing with yourself?, haven't seen your ass around.

CARLIN: You know, you know, I been where it's at. What you been doing?

ANGELA: Looking for someone like you, baby G. Aw shit.

CARLIN: So, what?, you just looking for me?

ANGELA: Someone *like* you.

CARLIN: Well, you found what you were looking for.

ANGELA: What you reading?

CARLIN: This? Nothing. Yo, wait, check it out, you seen one of these? This is slamming. *(He finds an ad which he has circled and cut out of a periodical)*

ANGELA: What's that?

CARLIN: I'm gonna get me one of these, what's it called? A Wizard, right?

ANGELA: *Wizard?*

CARLIN: Hey, I ain't gonna bite you, come on; this shit is everything all rolled into one, a TV screen, a phone, a fax machine—

ANGELA: 's mad crazy, huh?

CARLIN: —you write right on it, it recognize your handwriting and shit—Stop looking around, I'm the one talking to you, huh?—type up your instructions, make all the calls, know your voice. Someday, you come in, say, "Comb my hair, WizBoy," and he goes to work, turn on the lights, run the bathtub—I'ma get me one of these, save up, you can use it, too, right? What you say, you want to borrow mine?

ANGELA: Yeah. You seen Cashmere?

CARLIN: What you want with him? Cashmere? What's he got I ain't got?, *nothing*.

ANGELA: That's why you working for him then, right?

CARLIN: Working for—? Motherfucker takes orders from *me*, didn't you know? Working for him? Please.

ANGELA: What you doing with your ass in this park, huh?

CARLIN: I'm studying.

ANGELA: Uh-huh.

CARLIN: What's it look like I'm doing? It's a free country.

(Cashmere appears in the shadows.)

CASHMERE: Yo, Ange! Carlin, you on company time now, all right? *(He exits)*

ANGELA: Oh, you ain't working for him.

(Angela moves to follow Cashmere, and Carlin stops her.)

CARLIN: Yo, stay away from him, shit, you get mixed up in that freebasin', it gets real . . . *(He is searching for the right word)*

ANGELA: Who said nothin' about—

CARLIN *(Overlapping)*: Yo, it gets real—It gets *real*.

ANGELA: Yeah, you some little science nerd in your mind, Carlin, but you only got the nerd part down, you forget about the science.

CARLIN: Trying to get me to chase after you, that's what that is.

ANGELA *(Overlapping)*: No, you still playing with toys, sorry.

CARLIN: Yeah, I got a toy you can play with right here, girl.

ANGELA: Uh-huh, got you microscope? That's the only way we gonna find that thing.

CARLIN: Oh yeah? You be surprised.

(She is gone. Above, David enters the bedroom with his laptop.)

DAVID: Hey look.

(Aña appears in the bedroom door.)

JANET: 'Night 'night, beautiful, no more milk, all gone.
DAVID: 'Night, buddy. Mommy and Daddy love you very much.

(Janet hands the infant to Aña.)

JANET: Hasta mañana, Aña. Te veo en la mañana? Esta bien?
DAVID: Sleep tight.
JANET: Buenas noches.
DAVID: Hasta mañana.

(Aña exits with the crying baby.)

JANET: Oh god.
DAVID: He's okay.
JANET: Why does he always cry when he goes with her?
DAVID: Stop. Here, you want to see something cool? *(He brings his laptop to the bed, attaching a phone line to the modem)* I figured out how to get the news on-line. I just learned, you'll love this. Look. "Newstand!" *(He scrolls through headlines)* You see? Bosnia . . . School Closings . . .

(Carlin scoops up the newspaper and begins scanning headlines.)

"President of Disney Receives Record Salary" . . . Mmmm.
CARLIN: Shit.
DAVID: "Six Year Old Held in Slaying."
CARLIN: Guilty!
DAVID: "Lesbians Fight State for Right to Marry!"

CARLIN: They just mad 'cause they ain't getting any, you know that's true.

(Janet goes off.)

DAVID: Oh, I love this story, have you seen this? She's *America's Child* . . . And she and her lover live in Maine now . . . "The Lesbian State." It is, it says so on the license plate, I swear to god.

JANET *(Reappears, brushing her teeth)*: Mm-hm.

DAVID: And they're suing like all these insurance companies and everybody in the world practically and— . . . Oh, they're coming to town.

(He reads; Carlin reads the same article.)

They're getting an award. From GLAAD. Ohhhh, I'm glad. For being positive role models and fighting back . . . I guess . . . They're making the trip even though she's really sick. You remember her.

(A separate light has come up on a train compartment where Eleanor is seated, exhausted. Extremely ill, her head wrapped in a scarf, she is attached to an I.V. with a portable pump.)

JANET: Who?

DAVID AND CARLIN *(In unison)*: *America's Child.*

CARLIN: Fuck.

(Janet goes back into the bathroom.)

DAVID: They've had two thousand years of reruns, they were just on *60 Minutes* or something.

CARLIN: *America's Child* . . . a muffdiver, man!

DAVID *(Absorbed in article)*: Unbelievable . . .

CARLIN: They every damn place, right? What the hell happened? All on the same damn day, everybody: I'm gay!

Me, too! I'm queer, I'm a dike! Let's have a parade. Something in the damn water or something.

(Janet comes out of the bathroom.)

JANET: I'm sorry, who's *America's Child?*, I wasn't . . .

DAVID: Remember? Oh, yes you do, it was on for like a hundred and fifty years. They followed the whole family around with cameras and watched them take a pee and brush their teeth and—

JANET: Oh, oh, a TV . . .

DAVID *(Continuous)*: —we were supposed to be excited because they were black people—

JANET: Yes. Right.

DAVID *(Continuous)*: —and Look!

JANET: Of course.

DAVID *(Continuous)*: —They're just like us, except the adorable little girl at the center of it all announced she was a dike on her fifteenth birthday, and they were off the air in under a millisecond. Now she's got cancer, and she and her girlfriend, who's white, I think—

JANET: Oh, that's nice. *(She is rolling a joint on the bed beside David)*

DAVID: Why?

JANET: What do you mean?

DAVID: Why is it nice?

JANET: Well . . . is it *not* nice?

DAVID: No . . . They were beat up by a bunch of kids with golf clubs . . .

(Janet lights the joint and offers it to David.)

JANET: You want?

DAVID *(Taking it)*: You should read this . . .

(They look at the screen together; Carlin continues reading. In the train compartment, Barbara enters, winded, carrying their luggage.)

BARBARA: Uh! God.

ELEANOR: I wish we could fly.

BARBARA: I wish we could too. But it's sort of amazing that these sleeper cars still exist. *(She stows the luggage and begins getting settled: she cannot hold still for more than a few seconds)*

ELEANOR: I meant really. Really fly.

BARBARA: Oh . . . Well, me, too. But this way at least we can be private, and I actually thought it might be easier if we could stretch out . . . Did you take your pain pill?

(Eleanor nods. Barbara unpacks a videocam.)

Do you want another one?

ELEANOR: No.

BARBARA: You sure?

ELEANOR: I'd like to have some part of my brain functioning.

BARBARA: Okay.

ELEANOR: One part of me that works.

(Barbara aims the videocam at Eleanor.)

BARBARA: Look this way. Please? I want something to remember the trip; this time is precious to me.

ELEANOR: Then put it down or they'll find two neat halves of someone who looks very much like you, one on either side of the tracks . . .

(Barbara puts the camera down.)

Thank you.

BARBARA: Do you not want to go? Do you want to go back? The train hasn't started. Someone can accept the award for us. There's still time.

ELEANOR: I know.

BARBARA: We don't have to do this. I didn't make us go. I asked you if you wanted to—

ELEANOR: It's fine. Really, I love you, relax. I don't feel particularly photogenic.

BARBARA: Are you warm enough? . . .

(Eleanor is removing the scarf: her head is bald but for a few thin patches.)

You want to keep the scarf?

JANET: Jesus.

BARBARA: . . . No?

(The train lurches forward.)

There we go . . . Goodbye, cruel Maine! You want to listen to classical music? *(Pause)* You want to sleep? *(Pause)* Just sit?

ELEANOR: Read to me.

BARBARA: Read? Sure. You really look better, honey. I know this is tiring, but you really look good.

DAVID: Done?

(Janet nods; David scrolls through headlines. Carlin turns the page.)

BARBARA: You do. Okay, I'll read headlines and you say what you want to hear about, all right? "Oil Executive Brain-Dead from Bee Sting."

CARLIN: They probably just noticed, he been dead for years.

JANET AND BARBARA: "Babies for Sale in Central America" . . .

JANET *(Continued)*: Ohhhh.

BARBARA: "Artificial Intelligence Someday to Recreate Human Thought" . . .

ELEANOR: That.

BARBARA: You want that? Okay.

JANET: How do I . . . ?

DAVID: Double click.

(He presses a button. Everyone reads the same article.)

BARBARA: "Computer experts at the Institute for Artificial Intelligence believe they are more than halfway toward their goal of assembling a databank which will rival the knowledge and intellectual skills of the average American twelve-year-old child."

ELEANOR: Shouldn't be hard.

BARBARA: "The scientists began ten years ago by attempting to teach the computer, nicknamed Boy Wonder, the basic concepts necessary for an understanding of the *physical* world"—

CARLIN: Cool.

BARBARA: That's interesting—

CARLIN *(Stands, executes martial arts kicks)*: Boy Wonder!

BARBARA:	CARLIN *(Continued)*:
Up, down, right,	Up! Down!
left—	Left to the chin!

BARBARA *(Continued)*: " 'Hopefully, someday he will be able to distinguish right from wrong,' says Dr. Russell Farkas." *Right*, if half of Congress can't, why should he?

(Carlin resumes reading the paper.)

JANET: This is sort of amazing.

BARBARA: "Each day, Boy Wonder is asked to digest all the information published in three major American newspapers—" *Uh*-oh. "Any word or concept which confuses him—" Why is it him and not her?

ELEANOR: Read, please.

BARBARA: "—is cross-referenced and thoroughly explained. Earlier this month the computer shut down all operations in what programmers feared might be a total collapse under the weight of so much contradictory data. Within minutes, however, the screen lit up. Relief turned to horror as observers read the question posed by Boy Wonder . . . "

ELEANOR: What?

BARBARA: "Am I a human being?" . . .

ELEANOR: What did they say?

BARBARA: Isn't that sad? . . .

JANET: Mm!

CARLIN: That's wrecking shit!

BARBARA: It doesn't say.

ELEANOR: That's enough.

JANET: How do I get back to . . . ?

(David pushes a button. Carlin tosses the paper into the trash and returns to his book. Barbara has covered Eleanor with a blanket.)

BARBARA: You okay? . . . Wake me if you need me.

JANET: Oh my god—!

DAVID: What?

JANET: Oh David!

DAVID: What?

JANET: What's the name of those people on the fourth floor? Isn't it Hanson? She was killed.

DAVID: What?

JANET: She was murdered over on Washington Street—last night.

DAVID *(Simultaneously)*: Which apartment?

JANET *(Simultaneously)*: Right by the high school. Oh my god . . . You know who I mean; she's European? Or Persian . . .

DAVID: I can't—

JANET: They never say hi, you practically have to shake them to get them to look at you.

DAVID: That could be one of a dozen couples.

JANET *(Reading, skimming)*: Twelve- to sixteen-year-old black kid . . . made her and her husband—Carol and Reese, those are their names, that's them—get out of their car, took them into an abandoned building . . . He made the husband watch . . . Oh god, honey . . . He's in stable condition—doesn't say where. *(Short pause)* What would make a child want to do that to someone? A fifteen year old! Torture them like that . . .

DAVID: I don't know, sweetie.

JANET: And that's not that far from here, you know?

DAVID: If it were up to me we would move out of this neighborhood and go live someplace peaceful—far far away, forever.

JANET: If we don't read about it, does that mean it didn't happen? We always say, Here's another story about some other intractable problem. If any of us ever had even the slightest inkling we could actually unravel one of these headlines: how this could have happened.

DAVID: Uh-huh. *It's scary.*

JANET: No, but—okay, I'm stoned, but . . . get to the bottom of one single problem, why a *child* could be motivated to do such a thing.

DAVID: Yes. It would be fantastic, I agree.

JANET: And if *everybody* did that just once, in their *life* . . . whether they knew the people or not.

DAVID: Mm-hm.

JANET: And if there were a place where everyone could meet and assemble what they've learned . . . where everyone could *touch.*

DAVID: It's called the Internet, but—

JANET: No, it isn't, poor people aren't represented there. I'm talking about everybody! That kid outside and old people and . . . really rich people and . . . everyone.

(David has gotten off the bed; he is putting away the laptop.)

Where everyone's version of the truth, fuck you! . . . Where other people were real to us, that's all.

DAVID: It would be great. I agree. It would be incredible. I think it's great you have a conscience. I think it's wonderful.

JANET: But?

DAVID: But nothing. Do you love me?

JANET: Of course. Why do you . . . ?

DAVID: Just checking. Sometimes it seems like . . .

JANET: What?

DAVID: . . . we get stoned and you get all plugged in and . . . I feel . . . a little isolated, that's all.

JANET: Oh, honey. You're not.

DAVID: Are you—? I mean . . . are you unhappy with me?

JANET: No.

DAVID: Or with us? . . . Are you sure?

JANET: Yes. Absolutely. I love our life. *(Short pause)* I do.

DAVID: Can we sleep? I'm really beat.

JANET: Of course. Oh, honey, I'm sorry if I—

DAVID: It's okay. Sorry about the . . . what's-their-names.

JANET: Hansons. I love you. *(Pause)* I do.

DAVID: Sweet dreams.

(He turns out his bedside lamp. Carlin is stretched out on his bench, eyes closed. Barbara, leaning against Eleanor, closes her eyes. Janet lies awake for a moment before reaching to turn out her light. Nothing moves. Shadows deepen, lights change. Sound of a human heartbeat. Everyone is asleep. Barbara, Janet and Carlin are each in tight spotlights. Barbara opens her eyes and speaks to us.)

BARBARA: With the sound of the train tracks still in my ears, and the knowledge that this will be our last trip together, I dream we're . . . someplace . . . watching all this videotape of Eleanor: every episode of *America's Child*, all the stuff I've shot since we fell in love, like—*I know*, when your life passes before your eyes before you die? But it's *our* lives . . . Eleanor taking her first baby steps, tasting her first artichoke, the moment we met, the time we were attacked . . . and making love . . . And I realize: she's how I know who I am in all ways.

(Janet opens her eyes and sits up, speaking to us.)

JANET: I dream David leaves me; I chase him to the hospital, and I can't tell the difference between the patients and the doctors, everything's *white* . . . Then we're in this underground place and I'm breathing . . . smoke: it's a drug, and I feel transformed. Like seeing god before you . . . naked.

(Carlin wakes, speaks to us.)

CARLIN: Yo, I dream I get me a Wizard, man, bringing up screens, sending faxes, what you want *next*, man?, push the button! Here comes Carlin, floating in cyberspace, doing the freestyle, *anything's* possible!

JANET: Anything's possible: there are no more differences between people, no envy—

CARLIN: No more group home!

JANET: No more "haves"—

CARLIN: No more curfews.

JANET: —and "have-nots."

CARLIN: Yo, no more hundred bucks a week to sit here, do my homework, keep an eye out for cops, I'm out!, I'm up, up-and-coming, man, watch out, here he is! Straight down the information highway! *(He steers an imaginary spaceship)*

BARBARA: Then . . . suddenly Eleanor's not beside me anymore, and I look at the screen . . . and she's *inside*.

JANET: We're inside each other and see everything. We're one.

CARLIN: We're coming in!

BARBARA: Eleanor?!

CARLIN: I think I see it! There it is!

JANET: *This* is the world I want to give Nicky. So he doesn't grow up like that boy in the park.

CARLIN *(Hand over his ear)*: We're losing contact!

JANET: So that boy in the park doesn't grow up like that boy in the park.

(An object has begun to rise up from the floor in front of Carlin.)

BARBARA: And I can't reach her.

CARLIN: We're breaking up!

BARBARA: I can't get through.

(Carlin lands his vehicle; Janet and Barbara close their eyes and return to sleep.)

CARLIN: We're here!

(Carlin moves toward the object, kneels down, slowly lifts the lid: it glows from within, illuminating his face. Tentatively he pushes a button, and an enormous screen overhead springs to life with the words "Welcome, Carlin!")

OH, SHIT!

(He watches, mesmerized, then begins touching buttons, and image upon image, option upon option, appears above: a teenager's dream of cyberspace menus—flashy products, rap videos, phrases. These images flash by too quickly to read all the words. Carlin touches a button labeled "Love Connection," and Angela at once appears live beside Carlin, laughing as before.)

ANGELA: Yeah, you some little science nerd in your mind, Carlin, but you only got the nerd part down, you forget about the science.
CARLIN: Trying to get me to chase after you, that's what that is.
ANGELA *(Overlapping)*: No, you still playing with toys, sorry.
CARLIN: Yeah, I got a toy you can play with, right here, girl.
ANGELA: Uh-huh, got you microscope? That's the only way we gonna find that thing.

(She freezes as an amplified voice from overhead announces:)

AMPLIFIED VOICE: You choose what happens next to Carlin and Angela . . .
CARLIN: I do?

AMPLIFIED VOICE: . . . by selecting one of the following options. You decide whether: Angela finds another boyfriend!

CARLIN: No way, no.

AMPLIFIED VOICE: Carlin finds another girlfriend.

CARLIN *("No!")*: Uhn-un.

AMPLIFIED VOICE: Or Carlin convinces Angela to be his girlfriend.

CARLIN: Yeah!

AMPLIFIED VOICE: You want that?

CARLIN: YES!

(Carlin presses a button, and Angela comes to life again.)

CARLIN: Angie?

ANGELA: What?

CARLIN: I don't know how to say this, okay?, but I'll try. I think I could . . . I think I could make you happy. Don't laugh, okay? I'm just finding my way, too, right?, like everybody. I want to do what's best for you, for me . . . And . . . we could come strong . . . *together* . . . if you'll, if you'll be my *partner*.

ANGELA: Oh, Carlin.

CARLIN: What?

ANGELA: That was so . . . eloquent.

CARLIN: It was?

ANGELA: Shit, yes.

CARLIN: Really?

ANGELA: I didn't know you had all those . . . *words*.

CARLIN: Well, I did . . . I do!

(She kisses him, music swelling. Cashmere appears with a large potato chip bag; the screen turns to static, then fades to black; the glowing box vanishes along with Angela.)

CASHMERE: CARLIN!

CARLIN: What?

CASHMERE: Listen up, I need you to stay on point now, all right?, my first lieutenant just fucked up on me—

CARLIN: All right.

CASHMERE: I need you to run this down to the train station, deliver to a light-skinneded dude in purple hood and purple nikes, you got it?

CARLIN: What's his name?

CASHMERE: His name is Mr. Purple, motherfucker, don't matter what his name is—

CARLIN: Okay!

CASHMERE: Just do the job and you get a big bonus and promotion, but don't fuck up now—

CARLIN: I ain't gonna fuck up.

CASHMERE: No, you ain't. Bring back every cent he gives you, understand, I know how much it gonna be, so don't think about skimming something off. Business is business: Microsoft got their rules, we got ours.

CARLIN: I know.

(Cashmere produces a handgun.)

CASHMERE: Case you run into any interference.

CARLIN: No, no, hey, I don't need that, man—

CASHMERE: That's a present, man.

CARLIN: Yeah, I seen enough movies to know you—

CASHMERE: What?

CARLIN: Yo, you carry a gun, somebody gonna—

CASHMERE *(Overlapping)*: *What?* Motherfucker, this ain't no gun, this here a little piece of *clear*, you know what I'm saying? Yo, check it, everybody all up in your business, do this, do that, you got the problem solver on hand, make motherfuckers stop, listen up . . . You never have to use it, man but you always know you got it, right? . . . Your choice . . .

(Carlin takes the gun, tries its heft, then pockets it.)

Don't say I never gave you nothing.

(Cashmere and Carlin exchange a handshake, and Cashmere holds onto Carlin.)

I got eyes, I got one hundred million eyes like a fly, seeing everything . . . You do this thing right, I lend you some of them eyes, you see it all for yourself, yo, that's the shit. You'll see. You do it wrong, I see that, too . . .

(Cashmere releases Carlin; they exit in opposite directions as David's bedside phone rings; David wakes, answers.)

DAVID: Hello? Uh-huh . . . Yeah . . . Uh-huh . . . Name? . . . Oh yeah? All right . . . All right. *(He hangs up)* That's weird.

JANET: Do you have to go in?

DAVID: Uh-huh.

JANET: Ohhh, you do?

DAVID: It's him. Reese Hanson.

JANET: It is?

DAVID: He's in the ICU, I said I'd cover for them, shit.

JANET: What did I say? David, that's more than a coincidence, let me go with you to the hospital!

DAVID: No.

JANET: David, please?

DAVID: No. Go back to sleep. You're insane.

JANET: He's our neighbor, he's in trouble.

DAVID: Sleep. Now. I command it.

(He kisses her.)

Sweet dreams.

JANET: I love you.

(He exits. Short pause. Janet reaches for the remote control and switches on an unseen TV; the light plays on her face as, through the back scrim of her bedroom, we see the image of a TV screen springing to life. Janet surfs through silent images, arrives on the news, brings sound up on:)

FEMALE NEWSCASTER: —then fled into the night. Police say the woman and her husband may simply have been in the wrong place at the wrong time. A preliminary sketch of the assailant is based on the husband's eyewitness description.

(Onscreen: a crude rendering of Carlin.)

JANET: My god! Am I a total racist or is that . . . ? That boy looks exactly like the boy . . .

(She crosses to the window: Carlin is gone.)

(Simultaneously with Female Newscaster) He's gone! He disappeared . . . He couldn't possibly be the one who did it. Could he? No. *No. (Pause. As she heads out of her bedroom, she calls out)* Aña, wake up, I have to go out! Aña? Wake up!

(Under the above, continuous, low:)

FEMALE NEWSCASTER *(Onscreen, simultaneously with Janet)*: Anyone with information is asked to contact the first precinct. All calls are confidential, and a reward is being offered by the family for any information which leads to a conviction.

(Janet has disappeared into the darkness. The screen overhead becomes the view from a black-and-white security camera at Grand Central Station: Carlin, carrying the potato chip bag, descends an escalator. Carlin appears live, below, and the screen instantly goes dead. He crosses the stage and exits. In the train compartment, Barbara wakes violently.)

BARBARA: Honey? Eleanor?
ELEANOR *(Waking)*: What? What's wrong?
BARBARA: My god.

ELEANOR: Was I beeping?

(Sound of the train slowing to a stop; Barbara looks out.)

BARBARA: Oh my god!
ELEANOR: What?
BARBARA: We're almost there. I can't believe I slept the whole way. It's still dark. What time do you have?, my watch has stopped.
ELEANOR: So has mine.
BARBARA: It has? How's that possible? I guess . . . we'd better . . . god . . . Hurry, honey.
ELEANOR: All right.

(Barbara unhooks Eleanor's I.V., and the two women hurriedly pull together their belongings as the train compartment disappears. Sound of train announcements overhead as Carlin appears in a separate light; he still carries the bag of potato chips and glances around nervously.)

CARLIN *(To the audience)*: First delivery, right? Solo mission. Shit, I'm thinking everybody can see my thoughts, there gonna be metal detectors in the floor and shit, some cop gonna come up and aks if he can please have a potato chip. The Three Stooges selling drugs what this feels like: Larry, Moe and Curly Take a Trip to Attica. Nobody fuckin' notice me for fifteen years, don't start now, please . . .
BARBARA: All set?
ELEANOR: Let's go.

(As Carlin paces, we see him onscreen as if viewed from a security camera in a train station. He sits. In a separate light, a hospital bed glides into view, Reese Hanson wrapped in bandages, immobile, upon it. A night nurse—the same actress as Aña—enters, checks the I.V. Janet appears outside the hospital room, carrying her laptop and a newspaper. She hides until the nurse leaves, then slips in silently.)

JANET: Reese? Can you hear me? It's Janet Barnes from 15E?
My husband David is your surgeon. We live right
directly above you . . . the same line. Are you in 4E?

(He continues to stare out, never reacting.)

I'm so sorry about what happened. My god . . . it must
have been horrible. So unfair. I heard . . . that you
know who did it, you saw his face . . . Do you want to
talk about it? . . . Reese?

(Still no reaction.)

I can't get my mind around the idea of a child doing
something so . . . I have a little boy. And you think
about these things . . .

(Silence.)

You want to check the news and see if there've been
any late-breaking developments? I have my laptop, we
can hook into your phone line, is that okay? I just
learned how. Look.

*(She hooks Reese's hospital phone into her modem, then
pushes buttons. Below, a figure in a purple sweatshirt, purple sneakers and sunglasses enters the train station.)*

CARLIN: There he is: Mr. Purple.

(The sound of Janet's laptop connecting.)

CARLIN AND JANET *(Unison)*: Okay!
JANET: We've connected!

*(Carlin hands off the potato chips to the figure in purple
and receives an envelope in exchange; he feels its thickness
before slipping it into his pocket and glancing around. The
figure disappears.)*

CARLIN: Mission accomplished. Check to see nobody looking, no security guards, doo doo doo doo doo . . .
Check the time. Guess my friend ain't comin', oh well,
guess I just go home. Nothing special about me, no sir.
Oh, better just check . . . *(He takes out the envelope,
unseals it)* Shit oh shit oh shit, where's the *money*?!

*(He reaches in and pulls out pieces of cut-up newspaper,
then throws them into the air; they rain down on him as the
onscreen image above becomes on-line news: headline after
headline scrolling past in a montage.)*

JANET: There's the news, right as it's happening!
CARLIN: I fucked up, where the fuck he go? Shoulda checked
right away, which way'd he go, man, shit, motherfuck,
fuck FUCK! This ain't happening, it ain't, okay, breathe,
breathe, man, think, oh shit, I gotta think, think.

*(Barbara and Eleanor reappear in the train station with
their luggage.)*

. . . Okay, I'm outa here . . . I am *ghost*!

*(Looking over his shoulder, Carlin starts to exit and collides
with Eleanor, knocking her down.)*

BARBARA: Watch! Jesus Christ, she's sick!
ELEANOR: Barbara.
CARLIN: Yeah?, how you know I'm not sick?
ELEANOR: That's right. Sorry.

*(Carlin starts to edge away; Barbara pursues, first snatch-
ing the hat off his head, then catching hold of his clothing.)*

BARBARA: No! NO! Wait a minute, you apologize!
ELEANOR *(Under her breath)*: Stop it.
BARBARA: You don't just run into people and then—STOP!
HELP! HELP!

(Carlin pulls the gun, aims it at her head.)

CARLIN: You want it? That what you want, you dumb cunt?

BARBARA *(Very quiet, under)*: No. No, please.

CARLIN: Shut your fuckin' face!

ELEANOR: Barbara. *(She shields Barbara's body with her own)* We're sorry, please. We won't do anything. We didn't mean anything. We were attacked once—

BARBARA: Yes.

ELEANOR: —and we're both sorry, please. I've been sick, that's all, please don't shoot.

BARBARA: Please.

CARLIN *(Lowers the gun)*: Just about wet your ass, you dumb bitch. Blow you both back up inside your mama before you know what the fuck hit you . . .

JANET: Oh, this is a nice story, here, not what I was looking for, but:

(Janet clicks on a headline: "Lesbians Fight for Right to Marry.")

CARLIN: Hold up. You those big dikes, right?

BARBARA: *What?*

ELEANOR: Barbara!

CARLIN: You all getting the medal of honor or something for standing up and saying "We dikes!" And you *America's Child*, right?

(Barbara begins to giggle nervously.)

ELEANOR: What is the matter with you?

CARLIN: Shit!

BARBARA: I'm sorry, I can't help it.

CARLIN: Listen. I'm sorry I scared you.

BARBARA: It's all right, I have another pair of underwear in my bag! *(She laughs out loud at her own joke)* I'm sorry, I'm sorry, I'm sorry, I'll be quiet!

ELEANOR: She's in shock.

CARLIN: Yeah, well, me, too, you want to know the truth. Whoo, boy!

BARBARA: Don't tell me, wait, wait! This is the first time you ever carried a gun, right?

CARLIN: That's right!

BARBARA *(Explodes with more laughter)*: Well, you're one up on me!

ELEANOR: She doesn't react well to stress. Honey.

CARLIN: Oh, listen, we all just raised the way we are, right? To be afraid and shit. It's human nature.

BARBARA: That's right. Thank you.

CARLIN: People got all kindsa blind spots, you gotta work to improve your vision or else you stay blind, most people do. That's my experience anyway.

BARBARA: I am completely with you.

(Barbara has unpacked her videocam; she aims it at Carlin, who poses with his gun, proudly.)

ELEANOR: Barbara, now is not the time—

BARBARA: Oh, honey, he isn't going to hurt us, loosen up, we're alive! For this one instant we're not dead! *(She realizes what she has said)* I'm sorry, I wasn't thinking.

(Eleanor starts coughing.)

Ohhh, I'm sorry.

ELEANOR: Let's go.

CARLIN: No, you can't, you can't leave me here, shit! He'll kill me, he will.

BARBARA: Who?

CARLIN *(Scrambling to pick up pieces of cut-up newspaper)*: Oh, shit, I fucked up so bad!

ELEANOR: I've got to lie down.

BARBARA: We can't just turn our backs on him.

ELEANOR:	BARBARA:
I'm sick, Barbara, has that escaped your mind?	I know, I know, I'm sorry.

CARLIN *(Stands, moves to them)*: DON'T GO!
BARBARA *(To Carlin)*: I have to.
CARLIN: PLEASE!
ELEANOR: BARBARA!

(Barbara, torn, looks at Eleanor, then Carlin. At the same time, onscreen we see a headline: "Street Youth Breaks Cycle of Despair and Rescues Black Icon" along with a newspaper photo of the backs of Carlin and Eleanor, hands joined in a victory gesture before a large crowd. Eleanor, live, is having trouble catching her breath.)

JANET: "Street Youth Rescues *America's Child.*"

(Janet shakes her head and pushes another button; at the same time, Carlin has an inspiration:)

CARLIN: YO! *YO!*, I got an idea gonna blow your heads off, we could *save her life!*
BARBARA *(Putting down the bags)*: Save her life?
ELEANOR: I can't take this—!
BARBARA: No, listen to him!
CARLIN: Either of you ever heard of Boy Wonder?
BARBARA: YES!
CARLIN: Dr. Farkas and his—
CARLIN AND BARBARA *(Unison)*: —Institute for Artificial Intelligence!?
BARBARA *(Continued)*: YES!
CARLIN: They can work *miracles*, they know how to capture a *human being* inside a computer!
BARBARA: They do?

(Pause.)

ELEANOR: I'm going to the hotel.
CARLIN: Yes! YES, COME WITH ME THERE!
BARBARA *(Grabbing Eleanor's sleeve)*: No, I trust him.
ELEANOR: You're sleep-deprived!

BARBARA: I do—
ELEANOR: You're dreaming, he has a gun!

BARBARA: No, we've tried everything else, there's nothing else left! . . . I don't *care* if I'm dreaming, we *have to go* *with him*!	CARLIN: Here, take it, blow me away if I do anything wrong! Next time somebody try to beat you with golf clubs, they be surprised!	ELEANOR: Just *look* at him! Will you look at him

ELEANOR: If you don't let me go I'm going to shit my pants.
JANET: SHIT!

> (*Janet hits a button and Cashmere suddenly appears out of nowhere, slowly advancing on Carlin. As he does, Carlin sinks to his knees, petrified. The women are frozen throughout the following:*)

CASHMERE: I told you not to fuck up! You think I don't see you? I told you I got eyes, motherfucker—
JANET (*Frustration mounting*): Ohhhh!
CASHMERE: I see it all, and I'll find you, I swear—
JANET: I can't get it to stop!
CASHMERE: I'll hunt you down and peel the skin off your fucking face.

> (*At the moment Cashmere is about to strangle Carlin, Janet tries another button, and Cashmere freezes.*)

AMPLIFIED VOICE: You choose what happens now . . . by selecting one of the following options:
JANET: Oh.
AMPLIFIED VOICE: "Fifteen Year Old Held in Slaying" . . .
CARLIN: NO!
JANET: Is that—?

AMPLIFIED VOICE: "Fifteen Year Old Found Dead in Shootout" . . .

CARLIN AND JANET *(Unison)*: NO!

AMPLIFIED VOICE AND JANET *(Unison)*: "Artificial Intelligence Someday to Recreate Human Thought" . . .

CARLIN: THAT!

AMPLIFIED VOICE: You want that?

CARLIN: Yes!

JANET: I don't know . . .

CARLIN: YES! *PLEASE?!?* I won't fuck up, I'll never be bad. I promise! I won't . . . I'll be good, I swear! I WILL! Push the button, somebody!

JANET: Oh, well.

(Janet pushes a button, and the screen switches to fields of colorful abstract shapes devouring one another, regenerating, slithering out of sight. At the same time, the train station below is replaced by a mass of computer equipment, and Aña and Angela are now seen as laboratory workers in long white coats; they remove Cashmere's street wear, replacing it with a white lab coat as a pair of glasses go onto his nose. Cashmere is now Dr. Farkas, Director of the Institute for Artificial Intelligence. The scrim is removed from in front of the video wall. Throughout all this:)

JANET: Oh, what did I do now? What's happening? Everything's . . . changing! I can't . . . Oh, this is a *nightmare!* A nightmare!

(Lights change, and we are suddenly inside the Institute.)

CARLIN: Doctor Farkas?

DR. FARKAS: Yes?

CARLIN: Holy shit. You don't know me, okay. My name's Carlin Lane, this is, uh . . .

BARBARA: Barbara Barencki.

CARLIN: And Eleanor . . .

ELEANOR: Batois.

CARLIN: Yeah . . .

DR. FARKAS: Hello.

CARLIN *(Sees Angela)*: Hey, how ya doin? Whooo.

(Barbara looks up at the enormous screen and speaks in unison with Janet:)

JANET AND BARBARA: Oooo, what is that?

JANET: Isn't that beautiful?

CARLIN *(Overlapping slightly)*: Ain't it beautiful?

DR. FARKAS: Oh, those are artificial life forms.

CARLIN: That's right, Mr. Wizard here created 'em fifteen years ago. Right?

DR. FARKAS: Right.

CARLIN: And "They *still* just keep going and going and going!" Like pi when you try to compute it, never-ending, man!

BARBARA: Is that Boy Wonder?

DR. FARKAS: No.

CARLIN: Uhn-uh, this Boy Wonder right here, you standing *inside*—right?

DR. FARKAS *(Nodding slightly)*: I'm sorry, but—

CARLIN *(Overlapping)*: Listen:

(They listen to the gentle sound of the enormous database performing its myriad and mysterious tasks.)

That's his heart.

JANET: I can't take my eyes off this whatever it is . . .

(During the following, Janet drifts off to sleep.)

DR. FARKAS: We don't normally give tours on weekdays. If you'd like to call and—

CARLIN *(Cracking up)*: *Tours?!?* Oh, that's funny. Okay, you said in one of your articles which I happened to read on-line, okay, *if* you could ever find one single person whose whole life from birth to the present was entirely observable, you now have the means to synthesize all that data, right? *If* such a person could ever be found; Doctor, I'd like you to meet: *America's Child. (Carlin indicates Eleanor)*

DR. FARKAS: Oh, from—Yes, hello. A pleasure.

ELEANOR: Nice to meet you.

(Dr. Farkas shakes Eleanor's hand; she winces.)

BARBARA: She's frail.

DR. FARKAS: Ah, excuse me. I'm sorry, son, I still don't . . .

(Dr. Farkas suddenly realizes what Carlin is suggesting.)

. . . catch your drift.

CARLIN: See? *SEE?* I *knew* you'd get it! I knew it!

BARBARA: Get what?

CARLIN: You have an unbroken chain of information, chronicalizing her response to every conceivable situation over decades! From her TV show. All those years of video!

BARBARA: And I've continued to tape her, whenever she'll let me. Soooo—?

CARLIN: Okay. Tell them about your Personality Profile. Go ahead!

DR. FARKAS: Well, all right, I, we've created a program—fifty-five thousand questions which pinpoint your likes, dreams, fears, doubts, vocabulary—

CARLIN *(To Eleanor)*: He can create a database out of you!

ELEANOR: Me?

CARLIN: Everything in here— *(He touches Eleanor's head)* We can put in here. *(He gestures to the computer)*

BARBARA: You can?

CARLIN: We can keep her spirit alive indefinitely—as in *no death*!

DR. FARKAS: Might, little brother. Our work's still in the formative stage.

ANGELA: You're being too conservative.

CARLIN: Hey, I don't want no credit, it ain't about that. Okay?

ANGELA: I'm sorry to have to contradict you, but this is the breakthrough we been looking for, you know it is.

DR. FARKAS: Wellllll . . . It's a very remote possibility what he's suggesting—

BARBARA: *It is?!?*

DR. FARKAS: But—

BARBARA: *But what IS it?*

DR. FARKAS: He's saying that we can gather all this information about Ms. Batois and . . . recreate her brain inside the computer.

BARBARA: But what happens to her soul?

DR. FARKAS: At the moment of her death, it will seek out what it knows: Ms. Batois's brain . . . and it will find a home . . . *in there. (He points to the large screen)*

BARBARA: This is like a science fiction movie!

CARLIN: *YES!* That's right! We're making it up! The world, all of time, it's our movie!

DR. FARKAS: Ms. Batois would be sacrificing an enormous amount of her time with no guarantee.

CARLIN: You don't understand. She's *sick.* It's okay for me to say? See, this her *only choice,* and it's *real,* you know it is.

(Pause.)

DR. FARKAS: I never thought this day would come. *(Pause)* If she's willing to try . . . so am I.

CARLIN: Yes!

BARBARA: Honey!

ELEANOR: Wouldn't . . . ? Excuse me, but . . . even if what you're saying is true . . . isn't the disease a part of me?

BARBARA: No.

ELEANOR: You don't want it to be.

BARBARA: No. Do you?

ELEANOR: It's real, too, my cancer cells are real. They're . . . *mine.* Aren't they? Even— . . .

BARBARA: What?

ELEANOR: We're tempting fate.

BARBARA: Yes, we are.

ELEANOR: Even discussing this.

BARBARA: Yes, we are.

ELEANOR: Every human who has ever walked the earth has died, honey. We can't know . . . There's an order, a reason.

BARBARA: Oh, really?

ELEANOR: Look at the atomic bomb. We don't know what terrible *furies* we'd be releasing, by toying with nature, with the entire design of the universe—

BARBARA: That's right, and I don't care. We're fucking with god then, fine, he's fucked with us long enough, I mean, let him have it! FUCK HIM! *(She looks up, gesturing toward heaven)* FUCK YOU! YOU HEAR ME!

ELEANOR: Shhh.

DR. FARKAS: Watch it, sister.

BARBARA *(Overlapping)*: We're fucking you back! And we deserve it. So do you! We're fucking god.

ELEANOR: Stop saying that.

BARBARA: It's our chance! Please. I need you so. I can't lose you. I can't. Say we'll try, at least. What else is there? Please.

(Pause. Eleanor nods.)

You, what?, you *will?* You'll try?

CARLIN: NO TIME TO WASTE! Hang this up for me, would you? *(He leads Eleanor and Barbara out of the room)* Follow me. Hey, you the star again, huh?, that make you feel right at home. You gonna be okay, you'll see. Doctor, I'm gonna need you to help oversee the programming—

(Lights down on the Institute as David appears in the hospital room.)

DAVID: Jan? What's wrong?

JANET *(Wakes)*: Nothing, I couldn't sleep. Oh, but I must've; what a dream . . .

DAVID: You left the baby with Aña?

JANET: I leave the baby with Aña every day of the week.

DAVID: It's four-thirty in the morning.

JANET: And I know where my children are.

DAVID: You brought the laptop?

JANET: Please don't be angry. That could have been you or me who was killed.

DAVID: This is demented.

JANET: Something happened in our city, David, under our nose and to people we know!, and it may have been that boy who did it—from our park, the one we were watching.

DAVID: What?

JANET: Look, tomorrow's edition. *(She holds up the newspaper)* Tell me that doesn't look just like him. Doesn't it?

DAVID: Go wait in the lounge.

JANET: We can't just take the cops' word for it or the newspaper's—!

DAVID: You're *not* going to disturb that man after what he's been through. He's completely zonked on morphine and fentanyl, he can't hear you, even if he wanted to. Now wait for me in the lounge. Please. In the lounge.

(Beat. Janet turns and moves off. David exits. Lights up again on the Institute where Eleanor is being monitored with electrodes; Dr. Farkas, Carlin and one of the female lab workers are busily adjusting levels as Barbara reads questions off a laptop screen; as she reads, the same question appears overhead, enlarged. As Eleanor answers, Barbara types what she says. During the scene, Carlin drops off to sleep at an instrument panel.)

BARBARA: "If you had to eat only one kind of food for the rest of your life, what would it be?"

ELEANOR: Italian.

BARBARA: "If you saw a seven-year-old about to be run over, and you knew you could save its life by sacrificing your own, would you?"

ELEANOR: I think you'd have to be there, and anything anyone would say in advance would be self-serving.

BARBARA: "If you could return to one scene from your ado-
lescence, what would it be?"

ELEANOR: The day I kissed Eulalia Davis.

BARBARA: "Would you change any of what you said or did at
that time? If so, what?"

ELEANOR: I would hold the kiss longer and when it was over,
I would say, "Eulalia, that's because you're beautiful,"
instead of what I said, which was, "Wouldn't you like
some boy to kiss you like that?"

BARBARA: "If you had unlimited funds and no practical con-
siderations whatsoever, what car would you buy?"

ELEANOR: A Morgan.

BARBARA: "And why?"

ELEANOR: Because that's what you always wanted, and after I
go you'd have it. Type! Type it, come on.

BARBARA: I'm typing, I'm typing. How many more?

DR. FARKAS: Would you like someone to take over? Carlin?

(Angela gives Carlin a shake.)

Carlin?

CARLIN: I'm awake! I am.

BARBARA: She's the one I'm worried about.

DR. FARKAS: No, you take a break.

ELEANOR: Yes.

BARBARA *(Mouths to Eleanor)*: I'm gonna pee!

*(Barbara runs off to the bathroom; Dr. Farkas draws
Carlin aside.)*

DR. FARKAS: Carlin, you initiated this project.

CARLIN: I know, I'm sorry.

DR. FARKAS: If you're not going to keep your eyes open—

CARLIN: I know.

DR. FARKAS: —you won't see what's happening on the panel.

CARLIN: You're right, I'm sorry.

DR. FARKAS: Her strength is failing, we've got to try and get as much accomplished as we can; she's answered only a little over thirty thousand questions. Take over, and keep your eyes open, you understand?

CARLIN: Yes, sir.

(Carlin sits at the laptop and reads the question we see overhead:)

"If you had to explain to a four-year-old child that they were eventually going to die, how would you do it?"

ELEANOR: God. IIIIII would say that the body is a gift and that eventually we must all give it back.

CARLIN: Whoa. Okay.

(He types the answer; it appears above.)

"What is an algorithm?"

ELEANOR: You got me.

(Carlin types. The next question reads, "What time of day do you feel the most powerful?" Carlin, however, asks Eleanor:)

CARLIN: What . . . what's it like being famous? Is it fun?

ELEANOR: Not anymore.

CARLIN: It ain't?

ELEANOR: Is that the question? Is that what it says?

CARLIN: When people recognize you, you don't like that? Come on.

ELEANOR: No, I'm very private. Why aren't you typing?

CARLIN: You're *somebody*, you got it all.

ELEANOR: When I was a child, it was fun or novel to be at the center of attention, sure, but I would trade any of it, any amount of money or property, *everything*, to have what you have.

CARLIN: Me?

ELEANOR: Yes. Health. Time. A boundless ability to learn, to imagine, to laugh and keep on going. Don't think I don't see those things, Carlin. *(Short pause)* Now what's the question, please? I'll be able to help you more when I feel better—

DR. FARKAS: Carlin?

CARLIN: What?

ELEANOR: It's fine.

DR. FARKAS: What did I tell you? That's it.

CARLIN: No—

ELEANOR: He didn't—

DR. FARKAS: I said keep your eyes on the questions! Eyes. Like a fly. Seeing everything. A million eyes. Understand me, son? I think you do.

(Carlin stares at Dr. Farkas; Barbara returns from the bathroom.)

(To Barbara) Take over.

ELEANOR: I need to get some air.

(Barbara wheels Eleanor out of the room.)

DR. FARKAS *(To Carlin)*: I think you do.

ANGELA: Don't let him scare you; he's all bark and no bite.

CARLIN: Hush.

ANGELA: *You're* somebody, Carlin, you know you're my Boo. Huh? Huhnn?

CARLIN *(Overlapping)*: We have work to do, come on.

ANGELA: Don't you wish we could go away from here, just you and me?

CARLIN: I gotta concentrate on what I'm doing, Angie. I can't fuck up! Eyes. Eyes.

ANGELA: But when we're through here. You and me—alone?

CARLIN: Of course I do.

ANGELA: Away from Cashmere—

CARLIN: Cashmere?

(Projections of enormous eyes surround Carlin on the floor; he stares up as Cashmere's amplified voice booms out:)

CASHMERE'S VOICE: You do this thing right, I lend you some of them eyes—

CARLIN: What? I'm watching!

CASHMERE'S VOICE: You see it all for yourself.

CARLIN: My eyes are open!

CASHMERE'S VOICE: You do it wrong, I see that too.

CARLIN: THEY ARE! I DIDN'T DO ANYTHING WRONG!

CASHMERE'S VOICE: I told you I find you, motherfucker, I hunt you down. WHERE'S MY MONEY? WHERE IS IT? *HUHN?*

CARLIN: HELP!

(Carlin runs off into the darkness as lights come up once more on Janet, who's sneaking back into Reese's hospital room.)

JANET: Me again . . . We may not have a lot of time, so I thought . . . if there's anything you want to get off your chest . . . Do you ever feel that you're in some horrible nightmare, and everyone else is in theirs . . . and you can't find a way out, or even into theirs . . . If only there were some way to step out of ourselves . . . If we could just . . .

CARLIN'S VOICE *(Faint at first, echoing)*: Help!

JANET: . . . walk out into the blackness, find whatever is precious in ourselves and everyone, lose our isolation and . . .

CARLIN'S voice *(Growing louder)*: HELP!

JANET: . . . not be afraid . . . open up all the possibility in all of us . . . If we could just . . . listen for one instant—

CARLIN'S VOICE: *HELP!*

JANET: —instead of jabbering on and on and on . . . *hear* one another's pain . . .

CARLIN'S VOICE: *HELP ME!*

JANET *(Thinks she hears something)*: Did you . . . ? *(Short pause. She shakes her head)* If we could just—

CARLIN'S VOICE: *HELP!!!!*

JANET *(Slowly standing, following the sound of Carlin's voice)*:
. . . stand and . . . move away from all our own terror
and smallness . . . and call out . . .
CARLIN'S VOICE: HELP ME!

(She has left the hospital room.)

JANET: Hello? . . . Are you there? Hello? . . . It's all right! I
won't hurt you.

(Carlin runs out of the darkness.)

CARLIN: Hello?
JANET: I'm here! Can you hear me?
CARLIN: Yes!

(They approach one another in an isolated shaft of light.)

JANET: I'm right here.

(Carlin sees Janet, stops.)

Hello. I know you. I see you all the time. Do you recog-
nize me? I pass you in the park, doing your homework.
CARLIN: Oh, yeah.
JANET: I'm not who you were looking for, am I? Where is
she?
CARLIN: Who?
JANET: Your mom.
CARLIN: Oh, yeah, right.
JANET: What do you mean? . . . Where is she? Do you know?
CARLIN: I don't have a mom.
JANET: You don't?
CARLIN: No.
JANET: She's dead?
CARLIN: Might be.
JANET: What happened? . . . You can tell me . . . Please?
(Pause) No reason you should trust me, is there?

CARLIN: Ain't that, you go on.

JANET: No, I don't want to. I walk by you, never saying anything, as if I haven't seen you, but I have . . . You waved at me. Remember? We waved at each other.

CARLIN: Yeah.

JANET: So . . . we've said hello. It's a start. *(Short pause)* You know, it's scary being a mom. You're always afraid you're going to do the wrong thing . . . It is.

CARLIN: No, we talking about two different kinda animals here, believe me.

JANET: Okay.

CARLIN: Trust me.

JANET: I do. *(Pause)* It'll be between us. I mean, if you want.

(Short pause.)

CARLIN: Shit.

JANET: What?

CARLIN: Okay. That Casio was mine, all right?

JANET: Okay.

CARLIN: I paid three hundred dollars, it was 'bout this long, *longer*, and everybody always say, "Where's Carlin?"

JANET: I'm—

CARLIN *(Continuous)*: "Where you think? Follow the sound, man."

JANET: I'm sorry, Casio?

CARLIN: My keyboard, my Casio!

JANET: Oh, okay, sorry . . . Sorry. Go on. Please.

CARLIN: I worked weekends and after school, cleaning this man's apartment and shit just to save up enough—and people say, "How old are you, Carlin, twelve? You worked for all this money yourself?" "That's right."

JANET: Good for you.

CARLIN: Yeah, so okay, I come home, I'm like, "Where my keyboard? Hey, who stole my Casio? YO!"

JANET: Ohhhh—

CARLIN: I'm about to go out and beat the shit outa somebody, right? She just sitting there sorta: *(He imitates his mother, fighting back tears)* I'm like, "What's wrong, Moms?" She says, "I . . . I sold it" . . . I'm like, "You *what*?" I don't believe her, right? And she says, "I needed the money, I'm sorry." Five dollars, that's what she gets.

JANET: Ohhhh.

CARLIN: One time I'm sitting out front with my boys, right?, she—

JANET: Wait, I'm sorry, you have kids?

CARLIN: My boys, my friends, shit.

JANET: Oh, sorry.

CARLIN: That's okay. She throw open the window, right?, and start screaming; we look over: ain't nobody there. We're like, "Yo, Mom, over here."

JANET: Uh-huh.

CARLIN: Screaming at nothing . . . The last straw? She give my little brother, eight years old, you know what I'm saying?, and she send him all the way up on the subway looking for this man s'pposed to be our uncle or some such in the projects, right?, by himself she send him to go buy drugs . . . I don't care if she apologized, I got us out of there, and told the cops, too. I did. They got us out mad quick . . .

JANET: You did?

CARLIN: That's how I got in the group home, and I like it there.

JANET: Uh-huh.

CARLIN: I do . . . I don't feel bad about what I did.

JANET: No.

CARLIN: I watch out for me, keep stepping, that's what you gotta do.

JANET: Yes.

CARLIN: I'll never touch that shit, and . . . that's that, man . . . What about you?

JANET: God.

CARLIN: What you looking for?

JANET: Me? Oh . . . *(She shrugs, shakes her head)*

CARLIN: You lost, ain't you?

(She nods.)

Yeah, I can see that.

JANET: I keep thinking I'll find some . . . understanding. Or, I don't know . . . *justice.*

CARLIN: Yeah, you can forget that shit. God?—just some illiterate fool sitting at some keyboard somewhere, pushing buttons, can't even read the damn menu, he just messing with us, seeing what comes up on the big screen. Why everybody so sure he's loving and kind, "everything happen for a reason" shit. I say all the evidence points away from that.

JANET: Uh-huh.

CARLIN: Wouldn't you?

JANET: Yes.

CARLIN: He's fucking around, some vast fucking video game, and we the players. Nintendo! BLAM! There goes you, there goes me. That's all it is, man.

(Pause.)

JANET: You wouldn't kill anyone, would you?

CARLIN: Kill?

JANET: Not in a million years, even if your life depended on it.

CARLIN: What are you—?

JANET: I'm so grateful for this. I'll fix it, you'll see—I'll take care of everything! *(She starts to leave)*

CARLIN: Wait, hey, hey—

JANET *(Overlapping)*: You'll see, you'll thank me, you will! Sweet dreams! Don't worry, it's all gonna work out! It is! I promise you. Okay?

CARLIN: Okay.

JANET: Okay!

(Janet returns to the hospital room as Carlin wanders off into the darkness.)

(To Reese) He couldn't have done it, that boy, the one you said is responsible. I know you're lying, I don't

know why, but I know one thing: it's always easy to get the world to believe a black kid has gone bad, that's the easiest thing in the world; no one wants to see what's there. But I see you, I do.

(Reese slowly turns his head toward her.)

And you're awake.

(He lifts a hand to touch her face.)

I see right through you.

(He runs his fingers down her face, neck.)

We see each other. Don't we?

(He grabs her by the throat and begins choking her hard. Her voice constricts.)

Stop! . . . Don't . . . HELP ME! *Please!* HELP! *(She frees herself)* What are you . . . *doing?* My god . . .

REESE: What the hell kind of drugs have they got me on? This is . . .

JANET *(Overlapping)*: Morphine. This is a hospital. You're in the—

REESE *(Looks at her, screams)*: Go back! GO BACK! What do you *want?* I couldn't save you, you understand? I couldn't do it.

JANET: I'm not your wife.

REESE: You have no business here—Go back where you belong!

JANET *(Starting for the door)*: I'll get the nurse—

REESE: GO!

JANET: Let me . . . please . . .

REESE *(Continuous)*: You got what you deserved, now die!, DIE!

JANET: What do you mean?

REESE: For once and for all— . . . Baby, baby sweet Jesus I loved you . . . I'll always love you . . .

JANET: It's . . . all right, shhh.

REESE: Did you love me?

JANET: Of course she did.

REESE: Did you? As much as you loved to get high? Do you love me? DO YOU? *DO YOU LOVE ME?!*

JANET: All right, shhh, shhhh.

REESE: "I do believe in spooks, I do believe in spooks. I do, I do, I do!"

JANET: You're hysterical, you should sit down.

REESE: This is great stuff, *great!* Who'da thunk it, huh? *Morphine.*

JANET: Sit here, please.

REESE: Why don't more people opt for this?

JANET: I don't know.

REESE: It's cheap, it's legal, that's the problem, right there.

JANET: Sir, please—

REESE *(Unhooks his I.V. bag)*: Did you ever try *this* one? *Sweetie?*

JANET: I'm not Carol.

REESE: A little morphine, Not-Carol? Mmm?

JANET: No, you can't—Please, this is—

REESE: No? Just say no. *(He drinks directly from the bag)* No.

JANET: Nurse!

REESE *(Another glug)*: No.

JANET: You shouldn't . . .

REESE *(And another)*: No.

JANET: That's very dangerous. Nurse! NURSE!

(She tries to run for help, but he grabs her hair; he is standing on the bed. He squeezes liquid morphine over her face.)

REESE: Well, pick your poison. Oh, the *look* on your smarmy little puss: "A gun!" Thought you had it all, didn't you?, such a head on your shoulders, such beauty and brains—BOOM! "Where'd it go? WHERE'S MY *BEAUTY?* WHERE ARE MY *BRAINS???*

AAAAAA!" *WHERE YA GOING NOW? HUHN?* Gimme a kiss, *Beauty.* How 'bout it? Dreamed you went dying in your Maidenform Bra?

(They struggle, these lines overlapping:)

JANET: HELP!

REESE: How was the morgue, huh? *A LITTLE CHILLY?*

JANET: HELP ME! NURSE! HELP! SOMEBODY—!

REESE *(Continuous)*: Come on, one last little smooch. Aw, pucker up!

JANET: I'm not your wife—!

REESE: Hey, I wanna kiss the ghost. Mwa! Give me dead lips.

JANET: I'm not! Oh please—

REESE: I want dead lips—

JANET: I'm Janet. Janet, I'm Janet.

REESE: Lippies, lippy kiss, gimme lippy kiss . . . Show me you love me, come on!

JANET: We just, we live in the same apartment, that's, *please, please!*

REESE: . . . lippy lippy . . . Love me! Lippy!

JANET *(Closing her eyes)*: I'm *Janet!* Janet, Janet . . . I'm Janet . . .

(Suddenly David is there, dressed in his hospital garb, and Reese is once again immobile in the bed, staring out, eyes wide. David gives Janet a shake.)

DAVID: I know you are.

JANET: Oh. No, don't hurt me, please.

DAVID: Hurt you?

JANET: Oh, oh, I'm sorry . . .

DAVID: It's okay.

JANET: Oh god. He killed her! David!

DAVID: What? . . .

JANET: He killed his wife and said it was some black kid; he didn't love her, he hated her; he said it was because she didn't love him, but he despised her!

DAVID: You're frightening me.

JANET *(Overlapping)*: I don't know why, maybe she was doing drugs! She was, I think! That's why they were there. Do you love me, David? Do you?

DAVID: Of course.

JANET: All of me, though? Really, I have to know.

DAVID: What do you mean all of you?

JANET: I don't know, but all of me. The weak parts, the parts you disagree with.

DAVID: Of course.

JANET: Maybe I should meet you at home.

DAVID: I'm through.

JANET: Are you sure?

DAVID: No, I'm just gonna let all the people die. Come on.

(She hesitates.)

You're freezing. *Janet.*

(He leads her off. Lights up again at the Institute.)

BARBARA: Doctor? She's having trouble breathing, please, something is . . .

(Eleanor breathes short, rapid pants, eyes wide.)

I don't understand, she was doing so well.

DR. FARKAS: She's having what is called Cheyne Stokes respiration. It's the body preparing itself to die.

BARBARA: Aren't we ready to do the transfer? *Why not?*

DR. FARKAS: We haven't synthesized all the data; the computers are still working.

BARBARA: But it isn't fair. We've come all this way, and she's worked so hard—

DR. FARKAS: I know . . .

BARBARA: —answered all these questions, thousands and thousands, she's kept herself alive, for *what?*

DR. FARKAS: Carlin?

CARLIN: *America's Child* ain't all scanned, we can't—not yet, it won't work, I . . .

BARBARA: But how much longer would it take? Can't you keep her alive until then?

DR. FARKAS: Whatever you haven't said, whatever you need to say, you should say it now.

BARBARA: She can't hear me anymore.

DR. FARKAS: Yes, she can. She may not be able to respond, but she can hear you and she understands.

BARBARA: She's worked so hard.

DR. FARKAS: She's working now.

BARBARA *(To Eleanor)*: Honey? . . . I know I'm supposed to tell you it's okay . . . It's not. I didn't think I'd get used to this, taking care of everything, being the grownup for both of us. It's who I am now . . . If you die I'll kill myself, I will. Don't—if you see god, anybody holding out their arms, singing, "Come into the light," tell 'em to fuck off. All right? Can you see me? Look at me: you're still alive!

ANGELA: I'm sorry—

BARBARA: Do you see me, Eleanor, keep looking, right here, that's good.

ANGELA: You gonna h—

BARBARA *(Overlapping)*: KEEP BREATHING, YOU'RE DOING GREAT, KEEP LOOKING HERE, I'VE GOT A HOLD, ALL RIGHT? I'VE GOT YOU! GOOD!

(The screen overhead springs to life with the words "DATA TRANSFER COMPLETE." Carlin, Dr. Farkas and lab workers begin flipping switches, adjusting levels.)

CARLIN: There it is! Okay, okay, here we go!

ANGELA:	DR. FARKAS:
Thank god.	Just in time.

BARBARA: Do you hear that, it's almost done, we're almost there, don't stop breathing, keep breathing, look at me, Eleanor, I'll fucking kill you if you die on me now and I mean it, I'll chase you into heaven and drag you screaming back to earth and I'll make you suffer like you never dreamed of, look at me, say your name, look in my eyes, say Eleanor. That's right, Eleanor. *Eleanor.* Say it again!

CARLIN *(To Angela)*: Monitor ready? Please.

(Carlin pushes a button as Angela aims a remote control at the screen, which says "Not Reading Disk," before filling with row upon row of exclamation points.)

Shit.

BARBARA: Keep breathing, we're almost ready—

CARLIN: What are we forgetting? Oh, oh, pfffff!

(Carlin hits his head, "Duh!" He flips one last switch and the screen springs to life with the words "Welcome to Eleanor Batois!" and a bright, color photo of Eleanor in her prime—healthy and smiling.)

DR. FARKAS: There you go.

(The words "Check for bugs" appear on the screen, then a quick flash of photos of Eleanor from infancy until the present which rapidly assemble and break apart. Portions of the screen show report cards; the TV logo to America's Child; *a clip of Eleanor taking her first baby steps; Eleanor's high school graduation; Eleanor's newspaper clippings; Eleanor and Barbara's home in Maine; Eleanor on* 60 Minutes; *in a Gay Pride March, carrying a banner: "America's Child Is Queer!"; angry fundamentalists with raised fists and signs: "America's Child Disgusts God." There are X-rays, dental records, home movies, photos taken after the incident.)*

CARLIN: Beautiful work. *(He takes Eleanor's hand)* All right, the transfer needs to be timed precisely to the moment

your body functions cease. I know you know, and I
know you afraid, but you don't need to be . . . 'cause
we going to catch you and hold you strong . . . all of us
together . . . all right? You the star now. You the star in
our firmament. All right? You shine bright.

(Short pause.)

BARBARA *(To Eleanor)*: I'm right here.
CARLIN: May I have a reading on her heart rate, please? *(He
looks at Barbara)* Up to you . . .

*(Barbara crouches beside Eleanor. Aña begins applying
EKG leads to Eleanor, whose eyes remain open as the
screen overhead becomes her EKG. The EKG needle jumps
erratically, accompanied by a sharp beep indicating the
length of time between heartbeats, which grows longer and
longer.)*

BARBARA: I love you, baby . . . It's okay . . . I'm here . . . We're
all here. We're right here . . . Okay . . . Okay . . .

*(The length between beats stretches on. No one moves. The
needle makes one last jump; Eleanor has stopped breathing,
and a hollow, even tone has replaced the beeps. Carlin
urgently directs Angela:)*

CARLIN: NOW!

*(Angela pushes a button; everyone stares at the screen. The
flatline continues; no one moves.)*

BARBARA: Didn't it . . . ?
DR. FARKAS *(Under his breath)*: Come *on* . . .

(Pause.)

BARBARA: It didn't work.

(Pause; the EKG flatline continues.)

Just tell me. It didn't work . . .

(Carlin fiddles with dials, levels. Nothing changes overhead.)

We've lost her . . . Say it. Haven't we? Say it. I will. She's dead. It didn't work. That's all.

(Barbara turns back to face the lifeless body, lowering the eyelids and pulling the sheet over Eleanor's face; the screen switches to static, then Eleanor's lifeless face appears overhead, blurry at first, then coming into focus—a whirring sound as if some enormous database is purring into existence. Eleanor onscreen takes a deep breath and opens her eyes, licks her lips and says:)

ELEANOR *(Onscreen)*: I'm parched . . . May I have a drink of water? . . .

(Barbara turns to see the screen.)

(Onscreen) Could someone get me a drink of water, please?

BARBARA: Honey?

ELEANOR *(Onscreen)*: Yes?

(All look up at her face on the big screen.)

ANGELA: Mother of god.

BARBARA: Are you there?

ELEANOR *(Onscreen)*: Yes.

BARBARA: You're alive?

CARLIN: It worked, we did it!

DR. FARKAS: A miracle.

BARBARA: You're alive!?

ANGELA: Praise god.

CARLIN: Praise god.
DR. FARKAS: Praise him.

(Pause.)

BARBARA: Praise god.

(Eleanor's enlarged face stares down at them.)

■■ ACT TWO ■■

Lights up on Janet and David in the front seat of their car; David drives.

JANET: . . . Then he gets a knife or a scrap of glass and cuts himself to smithereens as if he's been attacked, he stabs himself a few times, too, shoots himself in the shoulder, bangs his head against the wall, stumbles out on the street, calls for help, someone finds the body, and who's going to accuse him of killing his own wife?

DAVID: Besides you, you mean . . . Baby, as much as I admire your, what do you want to call it, sense of civic responsibility in all this, you can't just barge into people's hospital rooms and start grilling them, I'll lose my privileges for starters. Look at this fucking road: the West Side Highway, where no one can hear you scream.

JANET: Have you ever been down this street? Turn down here, please?

DAVID: I haven't slept in two days; the baby's by himself . . .
(He turns the wheel)

JANET: Thank you.

DAVID: Why are we taking the longest possible route—? *(He realizes, steps on the brake)* No, nuh-uhn, no way.

JANET: What?

DAVID: We're not looking for their car.

JANET *(Reaching for the door)*: Then, all right, let me out, I'll walk, I'm serious—

DAVID: I'm sure it's been towed—

JANET: I'll get out at the corner.

DAVID: No, I have no idea where it was.

JANET: David—it's down by the school, they said on the news.

DAVID: Why are you doing this—?

JANET: We don't have to stop, but I want to see it, that's all. If it's there still, then we'll go home. I promise. It's already past five, you can sleep the whole day tomorrow, all right? Please?

(He resumes driving.)

DAVID: We're going back into therapy. Monday morning, I'm calling Buloff.

JANET: I have to understand. I have to know why she died.

DAVID: How is—? What if the killer decides to make a return visit? They do that, you know, come back to the scene of their latest triumph, relive all the gory fun and look for new flesh to carve up—

JANET: Try down here.

DAVID *(Turns the wheel)*: Sure, why not? What's sleep when you're with the one you love, about to die? *(He keeps driving)*

JANET: What were they doing driving around this neighborhood at this time of night?

DAVID: What do you mean? We're here, we live here, other nice people live here.

JANET: Nice people?

DAVID: Maybe they were visiting friends. Maybe—

JANET: Who are the nice people?

DAVID: Yes, nice people, the *non*-killers? *Non*-thieves? Being poor and abused doesn't always improve people, honey, I'm sorry to break the news. *(Short pause)* If there were such a thing as a lobotomy for the guilt part of the brain?, I'd treat us both to the procedure. Whatever it is makes people feel responsible for what they didn't actually do to other people, one snip and I'd have it out. I could make a fortune: "Come see Dr. Dave and lose your conscience, stop worrying about what you 'owe' society; snip, snip!, enjoy your life before they come and get you in your car, rape your wife, make you watch, blow her brains out in front of you and try to off you, too. Spend your dough on you and fuck the murderous, drug-crazed sons of bitches," I say . . . but that's just me.

JANET: There—Slow down, this is where it was, this is where she was killed.

DAVID: Great.

(They slow to a stop. Janet stares out as David locks the car doors.)

JANET: Jesus. She died right inside that building.

DAVID: Now can we go?

JANET: What could she have threatened him with?

DAVID: I don't know. Boredom?

JANET: Sh! Did you hear that? It sounded like something in that building.

DAVID: You smoked too much grass.

JANET *(Staring out)*: I've never noticed that, have you?

DAVID: Where?

JANET *(Strains to read)*: "Institute for . . . Arti . . . fffff—"Wait a sec. *(She starts to get out)*

DAVID: No. Janet, what are you—!?

JANET: For godsake, I want to *see* what it says.

DAVID: It's the middle of the night, and that's a *crackhouse*, now come back in—

JANET: And someone we know died there, so, oh, I know, let's walk away and do nothing about it. Great idea.

DAVID: We can't repair the entire world.

JANET: Why not? Why?

(Short pause.)

DAVID: I'm going home.
JANET: Fine. I'm going inside. *(She gets out of the car and starts into the building)*
DAVID: Absolutely not. NO, JANET, *NO!* STOP IT!

(She vanishes; David follows her. Their voices echo as if they're disappearing down an endless corridor:)

DAVID'S VOICE: Where are you going? Janet?
JANET'S VOICE: Look down here! My *god,* David!
DAVID'S VOICE: I'm gonna fucking kill you, I mean it! . . . Janet?!? Jan? . . . JANET!

(Lights come up on the Institute, everything as it was at the end of Act One. Carlin, Dr. Farkas, Barbara, Aña and Angela look up at Eleanor's face onscreen.)

ELEANOR *(Onscreen)*: I said, could somebody get me a glass of water, please?
ANGELA: I will. *(She runs off)*
ELEANOR *(Onscreen)*: Thanks.

(Barbara looks back and forth from the screen to Eleanor's lifeless body, face covered.)

(Onscreen): Say goodbye, sweetheart. I'm not there anymore, so don't get too gushy about it. I'm here. And I'm so *frigging sore.* Oh, man!
BARBARA: It's . . . that's really *you?*
ELEANOR *(Onscreen)*: Yes, if having six rats die in my mouth can still be considered me, absolutely . . . Oh, and I could use a shiatsu.

(Barbara touches Eleanor's body beside her.)

(Onscreen): Say goodbye and throw the baggage out, I mean it; I won't miss that broken-down piece of junk for one minute.

BARBARA: I will.

ELEANOR *(Onscreen)*: I know.

BARBARA *(Touching the body)*: So cold.

ELEANOR *(Onscreen, to the others)*: Maybe you should take it away.

(Aña moves toward the body.)

BARBARA: No!

ELEANOR *(Onscreen)*: Yes. Go on.

BARBARA: No, wait . . .

(Aña begins to wheel the body away.)

WAIT!

ELEANOR *(Onscreen)*: Barbara.

BARBARA: You can't go yet.

ELEANOR *(Onscreen)*: I'm here, I'm not there.

BARBARA: I know, but . . . *(Short pause)* Do you want to be cremated or buried?

ELEANOR *(Onscreen)*: Oh. Cremated, please.

BARBARA: Okay.

ELEANOR *(Onscreen)*: Thank you.

(Aña wheels Eleanor's lifeless body out. Barbara turns back to the screen.)

BARBARA: Oh. I'm so proud of you.

ELEANOR *(Onscreen)*: For *what*, all I did was lie around and moan for two years straight, really.

BARBARA: No, you didn't, you were very brave.

ELEANOR *(Onscreen)*: Okay, you're right.

BARBARA: You were.

ELEANOR *(Onscreen)*: Just—

ANGELA *(Runs in with glass of water)*: Here. What do I . . . ?

ELEANOR *(Onscreen)*: Hurry! Please!

(No one has any idea what to do next.)

CARLIN: Well, all right, I . . . Let me see. We should . . .

(He looks to Dr. Farkas for help; Dr. Farkas is stumped.)

ELEANOR *(Onscreen)*: Before my cheeks stick permanently to my teeth!

DR. FARKAS: We don't exactly . . . uhhh . . .

(Carlin is looking around for something.)

(To Carlin) What do you want?

ELEANOR *(Onscreen)*: I want something to drink!

BARBARA: No, we know, he— . . .

(Carlin locates the remote and begins pushing buttons.)

He's taking care of it right now.

CARLIN: We can reduce the size of the image—

(He pushes a few buttons, and Eleanor vanishes entirely from the screen.)

CARLIN: Okaaaayyy . . .

BARBARA: What did you do? Where is she?

(Carlin pushes more buttons: Eleanor's face reappears, reduced, filling only the lower corner of the screen.)

DR. FARKAS *(Simultaneously)*: Phew.

ANGELA *(Simultaneously)*: There!

BARBARA: We thought we lost you again.

ELEANOR *(Onscreen)*: I don't mean to seem ungrateful, but can somebody tell me what this accomplishes precisely?

CARLIN *(To Angela)*: Give me a hand.

(Angela and Dr. Farkas steady a chair as Carlin stands on it, holds the glass up to the screen in front of Eleanor's electronic mouth, and tips the glass. Water drips to the ground.)

ELEANOR *(Onscreen)*: You're kidding, right? I'm *thirsty*—as in I almost died!?

BARBARA: We're trying, honey.

ELEANOR *(Onscreen)*: Yes, you are. All of you. Very, very trying.

BARBARA: Oh, now I know it's you. You've got your sense of humor back.

ELEANOR *(Onscreen)*: Great.

CARLIN: Can't we mess with the programming and give her the *sensation* of having a glass of water?

DR. FARKAS: Yes.

ELEANOR *(Onscreen)*: How 'bout a gallon?

DR. FARKAS: We can do that.

BARBARA: But . . . will it still be her?

DR. FARKAS: Presuming this is her now.

CARLIN: Good point.

ELEANOR *(Onscreen)*: May I . . . ? Excuse me—

BARBARA: Yes?

ELEANOR *(Onscreen)*: Could all theoretical discussion be put on hold until we solve this?

BARBARA: Yes, he's going to do what . . . he just said.

CARLIN *(Pushing more buttons)*: I think we stored electrolytes on C drive.

(A list including Eleanor's heart rate, pulmonary functions and blood levels appear on one side of the screen. Carlin selects the blood levels, and a second list appears. From this he selects electrolytes, and we see a third list which includes potassium, bicarbonate, serum sodium, each with its accompanying current numerical level. At the same time:)

ELEANOR *(Onscreen)*: Even if it's not me, Barbara?

BARBARA: Yes?

ELEANOR *(Onscreen)*: Up here? Whoever it *is* . . . kindly requests that all decisions pertaining to me . . .

BARBARA: Be left to you.

ELEANOR *(Onscreen)*: And something else?

BARBARA: Yes?

ELEANOR *(Onscreen)*: Can I finish my own sentences?

BARBARA: Of course.
ELEANOR *(Onscreen)*: From now on?
BARBARA: That's the old Eleanor.
ELEANOR *(Onscreen)*: Old Eleanor is right. Oh . . .

(With Dr. Farkas's assistance, Carlin alters the numbers of the various electrolytes, and Eleanor's face visibly relaxes into bliss.)

(Onscreen): Oh, that's . . . *Yes.* Oh, that's much better. Now we can celebrate. Yay! Oh, *life*, living, no pain, I can't tell you.
BARBARA: No pain.
ELEANOR *(Onscreen)*: I feel like I could live forever.
DR. FARKAS: You can.
BARBARA: You will. *(Short pause)* Hooray!

(The others cheer. Aña returns with a cardboard box.)

Oh. Her ashes? So fast. *(She takes them, tenderly stroking the lid)*
ELEANOR *(Onscreen)*: Kiss me . . . Please?

(Barbara looks up.)

(Onscreen): Barbara? *(Small pause. Onscreen)* They don't care. Put it down now.

(Carlin takes the ashes.)

CARLIN: Go ahead.
ELEANOR: Please? . . .
BARBARA: I'm always afraid I'm going to get beaten. It's just . . .
CARLIN: Of course.
DR. FARKAS: A reflex.
BARBARA: It's so public! . . .

(Dr. Farkas holds the ladder for Barbara; she climbs up and touches her lips to Eleanor's.)

ELEANOR *(Onscreen)*: Thank you.

(Polite applause all around.)

BARBARA: It was nothing!
ELEANOR *(Onscreen)*: Could you ... Barbara, could you feel me?

(Short pause. Barbara shakes her head "No.")

BARBARA: Could you? Feel me?

(Eleanor shakes her head "No.")

Well, we'll always have our minds!
ELEANOR *(Onscreen)*: That's right.
BARBARA: Our spirits. We can *see* each other, can't we?
ELEANOR *(Onscreen)*: Can I ask ...? Carlin, I'm a database now, is that correct?
CARLIN: Well, in a sense. Yeah.
ELEANOR *(Onscreen)*: And if I wanted to I could, say, add more information into my storage cells or whatever they're called. Right?
CARLIN: Well, you can go on learning and reading just as you always did. Is that ...?
ELEANOR *(Onscreen)*: No, but you could also artificially plug me into electronic dictionaries and language programs, digital libraries. Couldn't you? Since I've been artificially assembled up to this point.
CARLIN: Yes, but then you wouldn't in the strictest sense still ... be *you*.
ELEANOR *(Onscreen)*: Right, right, but I'm not talking about that, I'm talking about what's possible.
CARLIN: Anything's possible.
ELEANOR *(Onscreen)*: Great. Then ... I want to do it. I want to know everything about *everything*. Barbara, if all you

have is my mind, then I want to give you the best one that
ever was or will be. I want to read the Bible in the original. Are there programs for that, that can teach me that?

CARLIN: Sure.

BARBARA *(Simultaneously)*: But—

ELEANOR *(Onscreen, simultaneously)*: I want to learn to play
chess, and soak up history and law, physics, my god,
there's so much to know! I've never even read the
Constitution, have you? Barbara?

BARBARA: No, I haven't.

ELEANOR *(Onscreen)*: I mean, read music, analyze baseball
scores, Chaos Theory, I'm finally gonna know what
everyone is talking about! I feel like I missed the newspaper every single morning for the last twenty years.

BARBARA: That's . . . no, that's all very admirable.

ELEANOR *(Onscreen)*: Say what you mean, baby.

BARBARA: Well—what? We went through all this effort, all
these months of trying to save *you*, not some . . . brilliant compendium of wisdom.

ELEANOR *(Onscreen)*: I'm sure you mean that in the nicest
way possible.

BARBARA: I've finally got you back, you're not in pain anymore, now you want to become something else?

ELEANOR *(Onscreen)*: Everything's always becoming something else. Isn't it? That's all there is is change. I've
got . . . I mean, to do something to fill up eternity.

BARBARA: Right. And I won't be able to keep up. I'll be lucky
if I learn one more language before I die. You have no
limitations: great. You'll be doing quantum mechanics
and measuring the Weak Force, I'll be looking up
"oiseaux" for the third time in an hour.

ELEANOR *(Onscreen)*: I'll always be with you. I promise I will.
Always.

(Pause.)

BARBARA: Well, *of course* we'll get it, all of it, whatever you
want. Sixteen modems! We can hook you directly into

Stephen Hawking's brain and you two can make math jokes to your hearts' content.

ELEANOR *(Onscreen)*: Thank you.

BARBARA: You're welcome.

CARLIN *(Bows his head)*: Lord, today . . .

(The others bow their heads.)

. . . with your help . . . we saved a human life. For all the lives thrown away through history, sacrificed in mankind's petty wars . . .

ELEANOR *(Onscreen)*: And womankind.

CARLIN: And womankind. His, and her, silly damn battles over this little patch of turf, that loaf of bread, a pair of damn sneakers, a silk *jacket*, a handful of coins for Christ's sake—Sorry, Lord . . . Lordess, whatever, shit . . . *Today* we finally saved a life, one life, forever and always. We praise thee for this gift, Oh Lord.

ANGELA: Praise him. Her.

OTHERS *(Overlapping)*: Praise him—her.

CARLIN: Amen.

OTHERS: Amen.

DR. FARKAS: I have an announcement to make . . . In recognition of the contribution he has made, not only to our friends Eleanor and Barbara, but also to science, and I don't think I'm overinflating his case, to humanity overall, I am very pleased and proud now to be able to inform you all of the promotion of Carlin Lane to Co-Executive Director of the Institute for Artificial Intelligence.

BARBARA: Oh, that's wonderful!

(Everyone swarms around Carlin to hug him.)

ELEANOR *(Onscreen)*: Congratulations.

CARLIN: Thanks.

ELEANOR *(Onscreen)*: No, thank you.

ANGELA: Oh, Carlin, let's get married, can't we? Please!

CARLIN: Wait, wait a minute, ain't that supposed to be my idea or something?

ANGELA: Well, how long you expect me to wait?

CARLIN: Well, I didn't know you *were* waiting, shit! Wasn't nobody gonna tell me? Angie, say, listen, I got an idea: Will you marry me?

ANGELA: Well . . . YES!

BARBARA:	CARLIN:
Ohhhh!	You will? All right!

ELEANOR *(Onscreen)*: That's wonderful.

CARLIN: Okay, we want you all to come to our wedding, okay? I can't believe it! How the hell did all this happen, holy shit. *(He looks to Dr. Farkas)* Ain't you gonna say congratulations?

(Dr. Farkas stares back implacably, then snaps his fingers at the screen. Half of the screen remains frozen on Eleanor's face; the other half fills momentarily with static, then shows the view from a security camera looking down a long, filthy corridor in a warehouse; at the far end, Janet appears.)

DAVID'S VOICE: Where are you? Janet?

JANET *(Onscreen)*: Look down here! My *god*, David!

(David appears onscreen, chasing Janet.)

DAVID *(Onscreen)*: I'm gonna fucking kill you, I mean it! . . . Janet?!? Jan?

(Janet disappears from the screen and immediately appears live, below the screen, inside the Institute; sparks fly from the Institute's machinery as if everything is about to short out.)

JANET: Oh.

DR. FARKAS: Stepped inside somebody else's nightmare, did you, little girl?

(David disappears from the screen and appears live behind Janet.)

BARBARA: Eleanor?

DR. FARKAS: Worlds collide and everything gonna break apart. NOW.

(Dr. Farkas claps his hands, and everything goes berserk: the Institute pulls apart; the screen fills with more and more static, portions of Eleanor's face barely visible behind a blaze of interference; one by one, the screens break down and go blank. Barbara fiddles with the dials and then runs up to the screen and calls into it as Eleanor disappears piecemeal. At the same time, Dr. Farkas strips off his lab coat and returns to his original appearance: Cashmere.)

ELEANOR'S VOICE: Barbara?

BARBARA: Eleanor?! Where did she go?

ELEANOR'S VOICE: Barbara?

BARBARA: I'M HERE! Eleanor? ELEANOR!

ELEANOR *(Onscreen, a faint signal)*: Barbara?

BARBARA: STAY THERE, DON'T LEAVE! DON'T MOVE, ELEANOR, YOU HEAR ME? I'LL STAY RIGHT HERE, I KNOW YOU'RE IN THERE, ELEANOR? I'LL BE RIGHT HERE!

(One small corner of the screen remains lit with static. Barbara kneels, pressed against it. Lights change, and Cashmere stands over the cowering figure of Carlin; he twists Carlin's arm behind his back, threatening to pull it out of its socket. Angela and Aña are no longer dressed as lab workers. They are all now inside an enormous room of broken machinery—monitors and a lifeless junk pile of obsolete and irreparable equipment.)

CASHMERE: Where's my money, motherfucker?

CARLIN: What?

CASHMERE: Don't play me, I want my money and I want it now! Where's the envelope? Hand it over, come on!

CARLIN: There wasn't any, it was empty!

CASHMERE: Oh, it was, was it, well, you better get the money fast, or you one dead piece of meat stinking up the trash, understand?

CARLIN: Yes, sir!

CASHMERE: HUHN?

CARLIN: Yes, sir! Yes!

CASHMERE: And Angie belongs to me, don't she? Say it!

BARBARA: Eleanor . . . ?

CARLIN *(In a burst of bravado)*: I decide what happens to me!

CASHMERE: Oh, you do?

CARLIN: *I decide!* OW!

CASHMERE *(To Angela)*: Who you belong to, bitch?

ANGELA: You!

CASHMERE *(To Carlin)*: Now you say it!

CARLIN: I DECIDE!

(Cashmere opens a switchblade at Carlin's throat.)

CASHMERE: Say it! *Say it!*

CARLIN: She belongs to you.

CASHMERE: Didn't hear you, say what?

CARLIN: She belongs to you.

CASHMERE: Who?

CARLIN: Angie, Angie belongs to you! SHE BELONGS TO YOU!

(Cashmere lifts Carlin and shoves him toward Janet and David.)

CASHMERE: Now do what you gotta do.

(Carlin reaches inside his pocket and lifts out the handgun, turning it directly on Janet and David.)

CARLIN: Okay, give me your money.

DAVID: Do what he says, whatever he wants, give it to him.

(David gives Carlin his wallet and takes Janet's purse from her, thrusting it at Carlin.)

CARLIN: One sound out of either of you, you're dead. All of it.
JANET: I know you!
DAVID: Janet.
JANET: We met in a dream, remember?
CARLIN: Your jewelry.
JANET: No, I have—I have *empathy* for you, don't you—?
CARLIN: Empty your pockets.

(David peels off his watch and hands it to Carlin.)

JANET: I know about your Casio, your mom.
CARLIN: The ring.
JANET: That's my wedding ring.
DAVID: Janet.
JANET *(Simultaneously)*: I can't believe—
DAVID *(Simultaneously)*: Give it to him. We can get another.
CARLIN: MOVE! This ain't your science project!

(Carlin aims the barrel of the gun between Janet's eyes, and she drops the ring into his free hand.)

Car keys.

(David hands Carlin his car keys. Carlin brings his stash of loot to Cashmere.)

There's your money, man.
DAVID: Come on.
JANET: No, I'm not leaving. I want to *see!*
CASHMERE: Congratulations. Little reward.

(He has produced a glass pipe and a minitorch, holding them toward Carlin.)

CARLIN: I don't touch that shit, you know that—get that out of here.

ANGELA: Beam me up, Scotty.

(Cashmere holds the pipe to Angela.)

CARLIN: No, Angie, come on—Oh, *shit,* come on!

ANGELA: Hush.

(She takes an enormous inhalation, then kisses Cashmere—tenderly at first, then passionately—before at last exhaling the smoke.)

CASHMERE: Excuse us, won't you?

(Cashmere takes Angela by the hand and they head upstage toward the shadows.)

CARLIN: Stop it, she don't have to, Angie, you don't have to do that! *(He aims his gun at Cashmere)*

CASHMERE: Put it away, man.

CARLIN: Angie!

(Cashmere unzips his fly.)

I'm gonna blow your fucking head off, be feeling around for your face and find a handful of brains, you hear?

CASHMERE: You buggin' out.

CARLIN *(Continuous):* I blow your dick clear off, motherfucker!

ANGELA: Ain't got nothing to do with you, baby G, go on home now, okay? I catch up with you later. *(She starts to sink to her knees in front of Cashmere)*

CARLIN *(Overlapping):* I mean it, I'm gonna shoot, put it back, put it back in your pants! I will—ANGIE!

(Carlin pulls the trigger: click. Pulls it again: click. Click, click, click. He lifts it to pummel Cashmere, who produces his own semiautomatic gracefully pointed back.)

CASHMERE: You think I'm gonna trust you with bullets the first time I send you out? Hold on, Ange. Just a sec . . .

(Cashmere zips up his fly and smoothly takes the unloaded gun away from Carlin.)

Think I was gonna let you handle all that cash for real? Had to see if you were trustworthy, right?, and you came through, flying colors; I'm gonna promote you in the morning, baby G, give you a big fat raise—

(Cashmere hurls Carlin to the ground.)

But let me tell you something, all right? This here?, right here?, during the day they do business, repairs, what all, and business rules apply. But after dark it's a place of peace where folks of like minds, interests, such as myself, Angie, all these people you see all come for a little R & R, whatever feels good, this is not a place for buggin', who did what to who, we let that go. You see all kinds of folks, too: rich, poor, black, white, straight, curly, nobody asks, nobody cares. We all united in a common goal, see?

JANET: David!

CASHMERE: And we work together; that's the meaning: *love* is the key.

JANET: That's what I was saying: a place where everyone could touch!

CASHMERE: Right?

JANET: Where everyone was . . .

CASHMERE: That's it.

JANET: . . . real.

CASHMERE: The world, see, everything outside is dying, okay? You're born, you live, you die. That's the natural law. You need any proof of that, just look around: This here your high-tech graveyard, the sick and dying fax machines, computer this, that, all the old TV's, turntables—remember records?—here they are, on their last legs, dinosaurs, right? Some lost civilization: United States of . . . Who? Can't make it out. One day all this shit was new. Once upon a time everybody opening up their boxes, Merry Christmas, oooo, whiffing in that new smell, seemed like it was gonna last forever, right? Here it is, months, maybe seconds later, everything busted, not even worth the money to fix this shit up. We gonna be gone—Pshoooo!, two seconds. Ghost.

BARBARA *(Thinks she sees a flicker on the dead screen)*: Eleanor?

CASHMERE: That's life. So this here the one, true demo-*crack*-tic watchyou want to call it where nobody be working their shit out all over you, you take that outside you want that, this the "Be kind to you, me place." The place of forgive, forget, we live and let live.

DAVID: Please, Janet?

JANET: They're just people, honey, people in a place.

CASHMERE: That's right. See?, now Angie likes what she about to do, but she needs something to give her permission; that's all that is: we don't make her feel bad about that. Touching, being good to each other, we all friends here, family. And love is the creed. It's the jam, baby. *(Cashmere tips his head toward Aña)* Now I bet little Miss Chatty Kathy over here will do the double master, if you ask her nice. You smoke, and she suck your dick, what do you say?

(Carlin hesitates before taking the pipe. He smokes it.)

All right? Don't burn your lungs out, plenty to go 'round.

(Carlin inhales. His face comes to life, and he sits up, staring out into the darkness.)

CARLIN: I'm god on this street!

CASHMERE: That's right.

CARLIN: I'm god. Why didn't nobody ever tell me about this? The world! *SHIT!* Look at it . . .

CASHMERE: Look, that's right!

CARLIN: I can't believe . . .

CASHMERE: I told you I give you *eyes*. Now *you* decide. You decide what Carlin sees!

CARLIN: ALL THE EYES, STARING BACK—
CASHMERE: Eyes!
CARLIN: LIKE JEWELS! A MILLION EYES!
CASHMERE: You decide, man, you decide it all! See what you *want.*
CARLIN: I feel the breath of god! I feel it, his breath! OH!
JANET: I want to try it.
DAVID: No.
CARLIN: That's the shit! *Fuck.*
CASHMERE: Come on over here, git yourself a little privacy.

(He takes Carlin into the shadows with Aña.)

JANET: I want to, David.

(Cashmere holds the pipe and lighter out toward her.)

CASHMERE: Go ahead.
DAVID: No.
JANET: Why? Please, David!
DAVID: The baby. Me.
JANET: Please?
DAVID: Your job. Prison.
JANET: I know, but I want it, please.
DAVID: No. No, Janet.
BARBARA: Shhh, you're gonna wreck my cloud!
CASHMERE: Your choice.

(Pause.)

JANET: No. All right, okay.

(Cashmere shrugs, takes the pipe to Angela.)

DAVID: I love you.
JANET: Oh, I love you too.

(Cashmere and Angela kiss, stroking one another's faces; then she puts her head in his lap and her hand in her own

lap: they make love. Barbara pets the dead screens, adjusting the controls.)

BARBARA: I see you. You can do it, I feel you . . . I saw you flickering, sweet baby . . . Come *on!*

JANET: Who are you talking to?

BARBARA: My baby . . .

(Barbara opens the box for Janet to see the ashes.)

JANET: Your . . . ? Oh.

BARBARA *(Retrieves the pipe)*: She was just here, she can't be—You can't destroy energy, can you?, it has to go somewhere . . . *(She flicks the minitorch and smokes)*

JANET: What was her name?

BARBARA: Is. Eleanor.

JANET: And you see her?

BARBARA: Talk to her, too.

JANET: Really?

BARBARA: She's learning *everything,* everything in the universe, and she tells me all about it.

JANET: She does?

BARBARA: Once you're off the earthly plane, you can see past all the things you thought were so important, you can see the grand design and all god's secrets—

JANET: You can?

BARBARA: She can! I can't.

(After her last inhalation, Barbara turns back to the screen, still filled with static, and strokes it, coos to it.)

Come on now, baby, come on! *Please,* I feel you, baby, I feel you here.

(The entire screen begins to glow, faintly at first, then brighter.)

Are you . . . ? Eleanor?

(All the other screens come to life, growing in brightness.)

Eleanor?

ELEANOR'S VOICE *(Barely audible)*: Barbara?

(Carlin, Cashmere, Angela and Aña all now approach orgasm.)

CARLIN *(Simultaneously with Barbara)*: Oh!

(The screens have begun to fill with dazzling, flickering pinpricks of color.)

BARBARA *(Simultaneously with Carlin)*: Oh my god . . .

CARLIN: Oh . . .

ELEANOR'S VOICE *(A little louder)*: Barbara?

BARBARA: I'm here! I hear you . . .

ELEANOR'S voice: Baby . . . ?

BARBARA: YES!

CARLIN: Shit.

CASHMERE: Fuck!

BARBARA: I feel you, honey, I'm right here!

ANGELA: YES!

BARBARA: I'M HERE!

ANGELA: OH!

BARBARA: Look out, look here! Come through.

(The rainbow of static suddenly clears, and Eleanor's face is revealed on all the screens; she is bathed in warm light, beatific, healthy once more, speaking out from every corner of the stage in a vision of indescribable beauty.)

CARLIN, CASHMERE AND ANGELA *(Breathing out as if one voice)*: Oh . . .

ELEANOR *(Onscreen)*: My god! Barbara!

BARBARA: What?

ELEANOR *(Onscreen)*: Did you know that the first Christian marriage ceremony, the first ever recorded, was for same-sex couples?

BARBARA: It was?

CARLIN: Yes.

ELEANOR *(Onscreen)*: Yes! Christ blessed all marriages.

BARBARA: That's . . . that's wonderful, how did you . . . ?

ELEANOR *(Onscreen)*: It's in the Vatican library!

BARBARA: It is?

ELEANOR *(Onscreen)*: Yes!

JANET *(To David)*: Do you hear her?

ELEANOR *(Onscreen, overlapping)*: They know all about it, but they don't want us to know.

BARBARA: Yes!

CARLIN: God.

ELEANOR *(Onscreen, sparking with more static)*: Wait, I'm receiving, I'm absorbing more information.

BARBARA: Okay.

JANET: What is she saying?

BARBARA *(Overlapping)*: Shhhh!

JANET: But I can't—

BARBARA: Shut up!

ELEANOR *(Onscreen)*: This—this . . . It's the Library of Congress! *(Nearly orgasmic with the intensity of insight. Onscreen)* Mathematics are an illusion!

BARBARA: They are?

ELEANOR *(Onscreen)*: God does not have ten fingers! She gave us ten fingers so that we could work in the decimal system, but the universe is not founded on tens, it's a trick.

BARBARA: It is?

ELEANOR *(Onscreen)*: It's based on . . . it's either two's or maybe . . . No, no, it's pi! Oh god. God is pi. Uncountable, *that's* the base, it's not binary, it's not— IT'S PI! God has pi number of digits.

BARBARA *(Not comprehending)*: Pi.

CARLIN *(His high wearing off)*: Damn.

ELEANOR *(Onscreen)*: Then it's not expanding!

BARBARA: What?

ELEANOR *(Onscreen)*: The universe. It's not expanding.

BARBARA: It's not?

ELEANOR *(Onscreen)*: Because of the limit put on physical matter and time by the speed of light which is a completely arbitrary number, I'm . . . almost positive, it *looks* as if we are, but that's assuming time exists, which it doesn't. It's all happening at once, always will be, and never ever happened!

BARBARA: What didn't?

ELEANOR *(Onscreen)*: The Separation!

BARBARA: What separation?

ELEANOR *(Onscreen)*: You and me and god.

BARBARA: God?

ELEANOR *(Onscreen)*: It's pulled together in one place:

(Carlin stumbles out into the middle of the room, dazed.)

CARLIN *(To himself)*: God's heart . . .

ELEANOR *(Onscreen)*: Yes!

CARLIN: . . . 's cold.

BARBARA *(To Carlin)*: You hear her too?

JANET: You do?

(Carlin does not react to them; he sinks to the floor, holding his head.)

ELEANOR *(Onscreen)*: Why are we afraid to die? To be nothing, to be . . . *where?*

JANET: What is she saying?

BARBARA: Shhhh!

ELEANOR *(Onscreen)*: What happened before we were born? Where were we *then?*

BARBARA: I don't know.

ELEANOR *(Onscreen)*: Why are we afraid to return to that place, our *first* home, *before* birth?

BARBARA: I don't . . .

ELEANOR *(Onscreen)*: It didn't hurt us then, did it? What hurts? What is the only thing that ever hurts?

CARLIN: Life.

ELEANOR *(Onscreen)*: That's right!

CARLIN: Fff!

ELEANOR *(Onscreen)*: *Life* is the illusion.

BARBARA: Life?

CARLIN: Shit.

BARBARA: What does she mean?

ELEANOR *(Onscreen)*: There is no before, no after. Life is the only scary thing in the universe. Where things appear to change. Time appears to pass, tides rise and fall, crushing, drowning, creating. But you cannot create that which doesn't exist.

BARBARA: Wait, I don't—

ELEANOR *(Onscreen)*: We are lucky to wake up from the dream, from life.

BARBARA: Okay.

ELEANOR *(Onscreen)*: We made it all to amuse ourselves: the suffering, pain and sickness, pleasures—all of history, the world, it was all, all a game . . . It's all right, Barbara. Let confusion be your teacher. Let it guide the way.

BARBARA: Confusion?

ELEANOR *(Onscreen)*: Trust yourself. You'll see. We are all one—

(Again static begins to fill the screens.)

(Onscreen): We are one and the same.

BARBARA: Where are you going? Eleanor?

ELEANOR *(Onscreen, overlapping)*: We are one!

BARBARA: Wait! Let me come with you!

ELEANOR *(Onscreen)*: I am always with you! We are joined!

BARBARA *(Overlapping)*: I want to be, take me with you!

ELEANOR *(Onscreen)*: We are one spirit!

BARBARA *(Claws at the screen)*: I don't understand what you were saying, let me in!

ELEANOR *(Onscreen)*: Forever, my love . . .

BARBARA: Show me how, wait!

ELEANOR *(Onscreen)*: We are one and the same. Always, I walk beside you . . . I hold you . . .

BARBARA: I want—How do I get *IN*?!?

(Eleanor's face is now completely obscured.)

ELEANOR *(Onscreen)*: I am within!

(One final glimpse of Eleanor is seen through a blaze of static.)

(Onscreen): Oh! I miss you, Barbara!
BARBARA: I want to go with you, WAIT!

(Eleanor disappears; the screens all dance with white pricks of light.)

That fucking bitch, talking all that mumbo jumbo to me, I could slit her fucking throat. "Let confusion be your guide," what the fuck is that? "We are one!" I watched *her*, I had to sit and watch her sweat and waste away and wipe up her shit, where is *she* now, where the hell's she gonna be when *I'm* the one screaming and . . .
CARLIN: Shhhh.
BARBARA: That's why I'm so mad . . . not 'cause I can't live without her . . . I told her this would happen, too, I told her. "Always be with you" my fucking—
CARLIN: Change the channel.
BARBARA *(Overlapping)*: I'll give you confusion, you want confusion, here you go, here, have her— *(She opens the box of ashes and begins scattering them in the air)*
CARLIN: Hey.
CASHMERE: Let her do what she gotta do.

(Barbara rips open the box, flings Eleanor's ashes over everyone and everything.)

BARBARA: Take her, she's yours! She's too heavy! I don't want her anymore! I can't carry her around . . . TAKE HER, THERE! TAKE HER ALL!

(She dumps the box upside down, hurling it to the floor; the ashes fall in a heap, a cloud of dust rising. Barbara wipes the ashes on her face, her dress.)

Thank you . . . Oh, oh, thank you . . . *(She licks her fingers)* Oh . . . take her, make her disappear . . . She's everywhere. *(Pause)* There. She's gone. Oh . . .

JANET: I want to hear what they hear.

DAVID: No.

(Angela lifts the pipe to Janet.)

ANGELA: Scotty'll tell you.

DAVID: No.

ANGELA: Everything you need to know.

DAVID: Please, Janet.

ANGELA: See yourself for real and true.

JANET: I want that.

DAVID: No, you don't.

ANGELA: Decide for yourself what you want to see.

DAVID: Janet.

(Janet smokes. The floor around Carlin glows as he faces up, eyes closed. Janet kneels beside him.)

JANET: I've been trying to get to you . . . Carlin? Is that your name? . . . it seems for the longest time. We're dreamers, both of us . . .

(He rolls away from her.)

No—Wake up, Carlin, we have to rouse ourselves—

CARLIN: Yo, come on.

JANET: We can't sleep anymore, we've all of us been in some kind of stupor.

(She shakes Carlin, lifting him up.)

        Tell me—

CARLIN: What?

JANET: —*please*, what can I do to help? What do you need to get out of here?

CARLIN: Out?

JANET: Yes.

CARLIN: Give me your money . . . Yeah, that's it.

DAVID: No.

CARLIN: Give me all your money.

DAVID: He robbed us.

JANET: Not all, but some.

CARLIN	DAVID:
Okay.	No.

JANET: How much do you need?

DAVID: Don't listen to her—

JANET *(Overlapping)*: Go on, ignore him.

CARLIN: To . . . what?

JANET: Whatever you need.

CARLIN: Go to a good school?

JANET: Yes!

CARLIN: Live in a safe place?

JANET:	DAVID:
Absolutely. What else?	There's no such thing.

CARLIN: And learn to use computers and have access to one and shit?

JANET: Yes.

DAVID: These dreams are useless, Janet—He's damaged goods, his spirit is soiled.

CARLIN:	JANET:
No, it ain't.	No, it isn't! LOOK AT HIM!

DAVID: He's not setting foot in our house, I wouldn't trust him around the baby.

JANET: Did you kill that woman? Carlin, tell me the truth.

CARLIN: No.

DAVID: He's learned to lie, it's too late for him.

JANET: That's what you want to think so it doesn't have to cost you anything! How *convenient*. Take one real look at him, David, he's been abandoned, he's real! Where is your soul?

(Carlin resumes smoking.)

DAVID: It's nice you care, baby, it is. Yes, I can see. He's paid a terrible price . . . Terrible . . . Now let's go home.

JANET: What did we ever do to deserve so much?

DAVID: All right. Fine. You really want to help, Janet? You really want to do something? For him?

(David goes to Cashmere, takes his semiautomatic. Carlin has resumed smoking.)

If he's innocent and goes to jail, what kind of life is that?

JANET *(Sheltering Carlin's body)*: Keep away from us.

DAVID: Put *one of us* out of our misery, I don't care who. Go on! You want to take our money and give it to him, because that's the only way you'll do it is over my dead body. You want to rid your conscience of his very existence, because you will never be able to shut him out, Janet, he will *haunt you*—then shoot him. And if you can't bring yourself to do either, then consign yourself to the suffering . . . or—

JANET: Kill myself.

DAVID: You choose.

(David holds out the gun. Janet does not move. Silence.)

You not only want me to say the horrible things, reveal god in his complete disgust for us . . . then on top of it all you want me to pull the trigger.

(David aims at Carlin, and Janet leaps to grab David's arm; Janet and David struggle over the gun, which she wrests from him; she points it at his face.)

JANET: All right, don't anyone move—

DAVID: He wants our lives, Janet.

JANET *(Overlapping)*: Shut up!

DAVID: If the shoe were on the other foot—

JANET: WHAT IS IT ABOUT SHUT UP AND THIS GUN YOU DON'T UNDERSTAND? *(Pause)* Carlin? I don't know what to do. Tell me the truth. Will you? You promise?

CARLIN: Promise.

JANET: What do I do? . . . I only came to help.

(Carlin shakes his head.)

What do . . . what do you mean?

CARLIN: I mean, you came . . . and don't misunderstand, like he say, if I were in your shoes I probably do the same . . . but I would say you came to feel better about you.

DAVID: That's right.

CARLIN: And that's okay, too. But . . . and I 'ppreciate what you would do, okay? . . . if you could, I mean, which you can't, so . . .

JANET: No. I— . . . I have to be able to do something . . .

BARBARA: You can't save anybody. Don't try.

DAVID: We're killing him already, Janet—slowly, inexorably like everybody else—

(Janet aims the gun again at David. He takes a step toward her.)

—including his own flesh and blood—

JANET *(Overlapping slightly)*: I will blow a hole inside your face so wide—

(David keeps walking toward her; she keeps the gun at arm's length, trained directly on his face.)

David!

DAVID: We've already decided that he doesn't count—

JANET *(Backing up a bit)*: I mean what I say, don't come any closer.

DAVID: —he's not worth the cost; we all agree.

JANET: To me he does—

(David reaches Janet and she lifts the gun, startling him, as she backs away, keeping her distance, the barrel trained on his face.)

Stop it, David, stop it now. Now!

DAVID *(Overlapping)*: The only question is how fast you want to do it. Now give me the gun.

JANET: I never loved you. I couldn't have.

DAVID: Yes, you did.

(He gently places his hand on the end of the barrel and turns it away, then slips his arms around her, enfolding her.)

JANET: No.

DAVID: Yes.

JANET: No.

(His hands are now over Janet's, which still hold onto the gun.)

DAVID: Close your eyes.

JANET: I won't. No—

(Together they aim the gun at Carlin; Janet does not resist him.)

DAVID: Don't worry, it's okay—

JANET: Don't do it, don't make me do it.

DAVID: Close your eyes.

(The semiautomatic goes off in a rapid burst of bullets; Carlin slumps over.)

See? All done. We did it together.

(David turns her away from Carlin's body; David and Janet are face to face.)

There. There, you're a good person, it's okay, shhh.

(He enfolds her in his embrace.)

JANET: I never wanted that.
DAVID: I know. You tried.
JANET: I never . . . We'll go to jail! David!
DAVID *(Overlapping)*: No. No one has to know what happened here.
JANET: No.
DAVID: You're free at last.
JANET: No.
DAVID: Yes.
JANET: It was wrong.
DAVID: Just say—

(She tries to look, but he turns her away.)

Come on, look at me—Nothing back there, look, say: "We're good," that's all.
JANET: But we're not! DAVID!
DAVID: Yes, we are, shhh—
JANET: No, I can't.
DAVID: Just say it with me, come on.
JANET: We're not. We're not good.
DAVID: Yes, we are, baby, it's okay. Look here: "We're good."
JANET: I won't, I can't.
DAVID *(Overlapping)*: Yes, you can. "We're good."

ANGELA: We're good.

CASHMERE: We're good.

DAVID: Say it.

JANET: No.

DAVID: You can. It's easy. We're good.

BARBARA: We're good.

DAVID: Come on.

JANET: I don't believe it, it isn't true!

DAVID *(Overlapping)*: You don't have to. "We're good," say the words . . . Just say them . . . Come on!

JANET: We're good.

DAVID: YES!

CASHMERE, ANGELA AND BARBARA: We're good.

DAVID: We're good!

JANET: We're good!

DAVID: Very good!

JANET: We're good.

DAVID: Very, very good!

JANET *(Overlapping)*: We're *very* good.

DAVID: We're very good.

JANET: We are.

DAVID: Yes. We are.

JANET: Oh, David, I want to wake up.

DAVID: Good.

JANET: Good!

THE OTHERS *(Overlapping)*: I want to wake up.

DAVID: Here we go. Come on . . .

(David leads Janet by the hand as Cashmere, Angela and Barbara all murmur "Wake up . . . Okay, wake up . . . I want to wake up . . . Time to wake up . . . Wake up now," lifting themselves from their torpor. Carlin remains prostrate, immobile, as the crackhouse pulls apart—the broken technology disappearing—and the three original playing areas reconstitute themselves. Janet is returned to her bed, Barbara to her train compartment where Eleanor is revealed, asleep. Angela, Cashmere and David all exit. Carlin lies still in his park as the lights change.)

JANET *(Waking)*: . . . oh . . .

(She sits up. At the same instant, Barbara opens her eyes.)

BARBARA: Wake up. Honey?

(Carlin sits up with a jolt.)

CARLIN: Whoa!

JANET: God.

BARBARA: Oooof. *(She looks at her watch, lifts the window shade a crack, flooding her face with sunlight)*

CARLIN *(Looks front)*: And the miracle, okay?, for that one second, shit!, 'cause it's *true*:

JANET: Jesus.

CARLIN: . . . is I'm alive! I ain't dead on some floor of some cold stone warehouse, listening to voices and can't even move, can't breathe . . . Uhn-uh! I'm here in this park, right where I was, never smoked no crack—

BARBARA *(Stretching her neck)*: Uh!

CARLIN: —touched no gun, never did none of that! Never fucked up. Damn.

BARBARA: My neck.

CARLIN: That was all some nightmare like you knew it was, had to be. Too true to be good, man, but it is! I ain't even late for school.

(Carlin stretches back out on the bench with his schoolbooks. Barbara has put on her shoes, and is quickly brushing her hair.)

BARBARA: We're almost there.

ELEANOR: Okay.

BARBARA: Take your time, we got time.

(The two of them begin packing up the I.V. and the high-tech pump, taking the bags down from the rack. David enters the bedroom.)

JANET: Hi. What time did you get beeped?

DAVID: Four or so, I don't know.

JANET: I didn't hear—or I must have, but . . .

DAVID: I'm glad you slept.

JANET: No, well, if you can call it . . . I dreamed I smoked crack.

DAVID *(Getting undressed)*: How was it?

JANET: Oh god, terrible. It was an awful nightmare.

DAVID: Sorry.

(Short pause.)

JANET *(Into the intercom)*: Aña, puedes traer a Nicky . . . Okay? *(To David)* How was your case? It wasn't that woman's husband, was it?, our neighbor, who was killed?

DAVID: No, he's at New York Hospital . . . Oh, long, brutal and unsuccessful.

JANET: Who was it?

DAVID: Oh, you know: another kid, shot up like a piece of meat . . . sister was there, sobbing . . . his aunt. Cops. The whole . . . happy . . .

JANET: Can I . . . ? I want to make a proposal, okay? Just . . . All right: I want to move out of the city.

(Short pause.)

DAVID: Okay.

JANET: I do.

BARBARA: Did you sleep all right?

(Eleanor nods.)

JANET: I'm serious. I know you've wanted it for a long time, and . . . we haven't really been able to save all the money we wanted, but I want to stop working and stay home with Nicky. I want to be a mommy for a while.

DAVID: What about Aña?

JANET: What about her? I mean, we'll find something—we'll ask around.

DAVID: Okay.

JANET: And she's a grown-up. Maybe you can even find a hospital out of the city.

DAVID: Oh, don't, it's too tempting to even think about.

JANET: But why? I think it's important for me to concentrate on us for a while. The three of us, that's all.

DAVID: I ain't complaining, I just . . . *Sure.*

JANET: Honestly, I want to lounge around the backyard and play with the baby . . . and smoke grass and not worry about the apartment being broken into anymore. Something terrible happening . . . I want to read and cook fabulous meals and swim!

DAVID: Wait a minute, who is this?

JANET: I do. I do!

DAVID *(Examining her playfully)*: Who is this woman? Really! Come on, 'fess up.

(He tickles her and she laughs as Aña brings in the baby and a bottle.)

JANET: Gracias, Aña. Voy a esperar para comer el desayuno—

DAVID: Morning, Aña.

JANET: —y David va a dormir, así que tienes que estar callada. Gracias.

(Aña nods, walks out.)

Oh god.

DAVID: She'll be fine, we'll find her something. She's an adult.

(Janet feeds the baby. Barbara and Eleanor are all but packed. The train is slowing to a stop.)

BARBARA: Honey? Before we go? When the time comes? . . . I promise to not be a baby and make everything about me, all right?

ELEANOR: What are you talking—? *Oh,* I thought you meant our award tonight.

BARBARA: No.

ELEANOR: I thought, "When the time comes" . . . ? You do what you do, okay? It'll be fine.

BARBARA: I love you, baby.

ELEANOR *(Smiles)*: I assumed so, it seemed like you did. *(Short pause)* Now move. I want my award. I deserve it . . .

(They continue gathering their things.)

CARLIN *(Looks front)*: The thing about dreams, see, is, and it's the thing I like about 'em, too . . . They real, like, *slippery,* you gotta work to hold on . . . They constantly like *(He grabs at the air, getting nothing)* Right? . . . *(Pause)* I figure, I stay in school, keep working for Cashmere, do what he say, get a raise, work my way up the ladder, never fuck up, keep saving, stay straight . . . get *out,* man. These kids buying coffins and shit like they aim to lose, shit, I'm coming strong, that's all there is to that. Somebody get shot next to you, you keep walking, keep on walking, that's it, that's all there is . . . Keep stepping. Right?

(Janet looks out the window.)

JANET: He's still there. Can you believe it? He was there all night.

DAVID: You can't feel someone else's pain for them . . . You can't . . . They have to do it themselves . . .

JANET: I know.

BARBARA: Wait.

(She takes Eleanor's face in her hands, kisses her, clasps her tight.)

ELEANOR: I know.

BARBARA: I know you know.
CARLIN: Wish me luck, man.

(Janet, Carlin and Barbara all look at one another through the impossible distances dividing them.)

END OF PLAY

DRUGS IN AMERICA

■ AN AFTERWORD ■

DRUGS KILL PAIN. Drugs make people feel powerful. Drugs keep you coming back for more. Drugs keep you from acting upon your rage and frustration. Drugs are useful. Here are some really strong drugs, hardest to kick: nicotine, crack, Valium, alcohol, heroin, crystal, *AOL* (*All My Children*).

Everything conspires to disconnect us. One used to have to see the bank teller, look them in the face, reach out to their hand—now it's a machine. One used to go to the movies, sit in the dark, laugh and cry next to strangers—now it's video rentals, cable. The mail used to arrive via a human being—now there's e-mail, faxes. (Who can bother to wait for snail mail?) One used to go to town meetings, to *vote*! One used to date. Now there's Internet and Cybersex.

Queer-critics criticize queer-artists for not representing their experience "properly." Powerful black voices are termed "intellectually light." Everybody wants to see a "positive" version of their own subset—all the options and possibilities laid out like a brochure for some bright future or a trip to Holland. Where are the tulips? We are depressed and enraged by anyone else's version of the "truth." Whose truth is it, anyway? An army of hip movie critics rave about *Pulp Fiction* —belly laughs rock the theatre as brains blast out of skulls, drug dealers die much-deserved Grand Guignol deaths, needles are plunged into hearts. The homosexual-rapists get just what's coming to them. TV sends a constant message that all of life is commerce. Every few minutes the story, the ball game, the news—*everything*, stops so that someone can try and sell us something. Even the deaths in Rwanda, in Bosnia, must pause now in order for Americans to contemplate new cars, new coffees, new beers. In whose interest should the disenfranchised remain benumbed by their daily infusions of *Loving*, freebase, Budweiser and O.J.? Nearly everything we see and hear in our reactionary epoch recommends further cynicism and contempt. Keep your reverence, your awe, to yourself.

One must travel a vast distance across the long and twisted highways of class, race, gender, sexual orientation, language skills and culture in order to reach the far corners, all the varied segments of America. From one's cloistered room, one's ghetto—be it the suburbs, the East Village, academia, a luxury high rise or a homeless shelter—all other noises are potentially confusing, enraging. Why won't they be quiet? Their numbers are so stupid, their values so corrupt. Why must they be so . . . straight, white, black, gay, poor, *lucky*? Why must the homosexuals want to march with the Irish? Why must the people on the street be so loud? Why won't they speak English? Why can't they turn down their car radios? How many people truly revel, *delight*, in our differences, distinctions, the crazed panoply of human expression? Uniformity is comforting. It gives the illusion of power—another potent drug. If all your neighbors agree with you, life is less scary. Power is agreement, agreement is power.

The pervasive moralizing about drugs—throwing people in jail, criminalizing their activities—has accomplished one thing with great force—driving the price of drugs ever skyward. This has certainly been the most effective achievement in our "war on drugs." Cocaine is the ultimate cash crop in a free-market economy. Fact: after food and oil, drugs and weapons (much of them manufactured in the U.S.) are the most heavily traded goods worldwide.

It certainly is not as if we as a nation have had no experience criminalizing intoxicants. Prohibition was a long and expensive experiment which created a criminal underclass, not to mention social hypocrisy (Everybody takes a drink now and then, right?), which we are now repeating on a grander, more grotesque scale. Even our president tried marijuana, though of course he didn't inhale.

Who protests the loudest when legalization of drugs is proposed? Congress, bureaucrats, the owners of newspapers. One has to at least ask the questions: How much worse could it be than it already is? What is everyone's *investment* in maintaining this particular status quo? Why, when any prominent official suggests we begin studying the possible effects of legalizing certain drugs, are they instantly silenced, if not fired outright? Certainly I am not the first person to notice that drugs pour into the U.S. from those countries in which the CIA has recently conducted "undercover missions"—Southeast Asia, Guatemala, Afghanistan, Colombia, Panama, Nicaragua.

Our leaders say we can't afford any more social programs, that they don't "work" anyway. (Here is what Clinton proposes we spend on defense next year: $256 billion.)

When was our nation poorer than in the Great Depression, and when were the most progressive steps in our history taken to provide a safety net for the elderly, the infirm, the unemployed? By shutting down mental hospitals, shelters and clinics, by absolving ourselves of all responsibility, what kind of a nation will we end up with? By giving more and more tax incentives to corporations, by allowing the richest Americans to leave our shores, pay no taxes whatsoever and continue reaping profits in the trillions, we have made our priorities clear. To those unlucky or stupid enough to have been born into poverty we say: we can't afford to educate you as well as the wealthy children (they can go to private schools) or keep you safe on your streets or maintain affirmative action principles (which are unfair, after all) or even to pay for your health care. Congress and President Clinton seriously debated covering ninety-four percent of our populace . . . the other six percent? . . . They must fend for themselves. One wished so very much that Congress would have to decide which six percent of their own members would go uninsured . . . which of their children should have to do without immunization for polio. As a final coup de grace, and with our Democratic president's approval, we have removed the last net protecting our most helpless citizens—poor children of single mothers—from utter ruin.

The United States has a higher percentage of its own citizens behind bars than any other industrialized nation. Three strikes and you're out. We are building more prisons as you read this.

As Peter Jennings says, your money, your choice.

What exactly is our responsibility to other people? To what degree are we obligated to provide for them? Shouldn't they take care of themselves? As a nation we are locked in a debate on this subject, led on the right by Elizabeth Dole, Tom DeLay, Trent Lott and Governor Bush . . . and led on the left by . . . ?

Speak now, or forever hold your peace.

—CRAIG LUCAS
April 1999

CRAIG LUCAS is author of *Missing Persons, Reckless, Three Postcards* (with composer/lyricist Craig Carnelia), *Prelude to a Kiss, God's Heart, The Dying Gaul* and *Savage Light* (with David Schulner). His screenplays include *Longtime Companion, Prelude to a Kiss, Reckless* and *Blue Window*. With director Norman René he created the bookless musical *Marry Me a Little*, with songs by Stephen Sondheim. He has written two opera libretti for composer Gerald Busby, *Orpheus in Love* and *Breedlove*.

Lucas recently completed the book for a musical, written with the rock band, Queen; the book to a musical based on the movie *Don Juan DeMarco*; and a screenplay based on Randy Shilt's biography of Harvey Milk, *The Mayor of Castro Street*, for HBO.

Lucas is the recipient of the first George and Elisabeth Marton Award, the L.A. Drama Critics Award, Drama-Logue and OBIE awards, the Outer Critic's Circle Award and the Burns Mantle Best Musical Award. He has been nominated three times for the Drama Desk Award, once for the Tony Award, and has been a Pulitzer Prize finalist. He has received two Rockefeller Foundation grants, a Guggenheim fellowship and an NEA/TCG Fellowship (at Seattle Repertory Theatre).

He has been awarded new play commissions from South Coast Repertory, Actors Theatre of Louisville, Hartford Stage Company and Seattle Repertory.

He is a contributing editor to *Bomb* magazine. His essays have also appeared in *The Advocate, The Dramatists Guild Quarterly, American Theatre, Frontiers* and *Lincoln Center Review*, as well as in the anthologies *Two Hearts Desired* and *Gay Men at the Millennium* and many others. He is a member of The Dramatists Guild, PEN, the Writers Guild of America East and the A.C.L.U.

A graduate of Boston University, where he studied with poet Anne Sexton and historian Howard Zinn, he lives in upstate New York, and is partners with set designer, John McDermott.